Maryland – 1980

Regulation, Values and the Public Interest

Regulation, Values and the Public Interest

Kenneth M. Sayre

Ellen L. Maher

Peri E. Arnold

Kenneth E. Goodpaster

Robert E. Rodes

James B. Stewart

The Philosophic Institute

University of Notre Dame

Library of Congress Cataloging in Publication Data

Notre Dame, Ind. University. Philosophic Institute.
    Regulation, values, and the public interest.

    "A report of a study undertaken during 1977-78 of the
social, environmental, and professional values of the
Illinois Commerce Commission."
    Includes index.
    1. Illinois. Commerce Commission. 2. Public
utilities--Illinois. I. Sayre, Kenneth M., 1928-
II. Title.
HD2767.I54N67   1980   353.97730087   80-451
ISBN 0-268-01607-0

Foreword

Utility regulators make decisions daily. Some of these decisions, such as rate cases and siting of energy facilities involve highly complicated matters which have significant effect on the public.

How these decisions are reached was and still is often obscured from the ratepayers' and utilities' view because they are made during closed commission meetings. Now more and more commissions have opened their meetings to the public either voluntarily or in response to a "sunshine" law. But perceptions of how those decisions have been reached have become fixed.

By and large, I believe the public, i.e., the ratepayers, perceive the regulators as "captives" of the regulated. Regulators, by and large, accepted this as an occupational hazard but one that did not pose a danger to their position since energy was inexpensive and the costs relatively stable during the 1950's and 1960's. Commissions during this period were not the focus of attention for the media or consumer groups. However, since the early 1970's energy costs, particularly electric energy rates, have been escalating at a pace higher than the general inflation rate. Many ratepayers now find it difficult or impossible to meet the cost of this basic necessity. It is not unnatural for these people

to come to the conclusion that only a group biased
in favor of the utility would bring such calamity
into their lives. The charge that regulators are
biased in favor of or controlled by the utilities is
now something more than an occupational hazard that
can be ignored. More than objectivity is demanded
of regulators by certain special interest groups. A
social philosophy that encourages lifeline rates,
bans on disconnections, etc., is considered an essential qualification to hold office. Anatagonism toward industry positions regardless of their merits,
becomes the litmus test to determine if a regulator
has been "captured."

On the other hand, the utility industry probably views the decision process as one in which external elements, politics, social concerns, etc.,
play too big a role; that the interests--legitimate
interests--of the company are not given sufficient
consideration; that short-term expediencies override
the long-term best interests of the ratepayer as well.

To a great extent the public perception has been
reinforced by some academic observers of regulation,
as this study points out. Too much contact has made
the regulators "sympathetic" to the needs of the utilities and eventually results in the regulator being
"captured" by the regulated. This allegation did not
attract too much attention outside academia until the
last 10 years. Now, however, every critical decision
is microscopically examined to determine the outside
influences brought to bear on the Commission.

The regulator, governed and restricted by a
statute that establishes the general regulatory frame-
work within which he must act, finds himself and (more
and more) herself in the center of this maelstrom
with its power intensifying every year. The respite
from rate cases grows shorter, the issues more complicated, and the emotions of those involved more
intense. There is not much time, if any, for a regulator to conduct an introspectove examination of what
values he or she holds that consciously or subcon-
sciously affect his or her decisions.

Despite this increased attention focused on regulation, there is an absence in the present literature of studies that measure the basic values of re-

gulators,[1] studies that might test the regulatory
theory, among others, that regulators become "captured" by the industry, This study and report by the
University of Notre Dame therefore comes at an oppor-
tune time.

Naturally, I am pleased the study concluded
with reference to the Illinois Commerce Commission
that "a considerable number of regulators [staff and
commissioners] in the sample are not aligned [with
the regulated industry] in any sense within their
control." I suspect this would be true with most
utility regulators. I would hope the study could be
expanded to include a majority of state utility commissions and I would urge the commissions to cooperate with the study team.

Finally, I wish to compliment Prof. Kenneth
Sayre and his entire team for undertaking this study
and for conducting it in such a competent and professional manner.

> Marvin S. Lieberman
> Past Chairman,
> Illinois Commerce Commission

NOTE

1. Perhaps the most in-depth study of the values
of regulators is done by the financial analysts who
rate regulatory bodies. Not only are the analysts
interested in the attitudes of regulators towards regulatory issues, but they become amateur "psychiatrists"
probing for the fundamental values which might adversely affect the financial viability of the utility companies. The results of this subjective inquiry are
seldom, if ever, made public.

Contents

Introduction

This is a report of a study undertaken during 1977-78 of the social, environmental and professional values of the Illinois Commerce Commission.

Why is a study of the value-orientation of a particular state regulatory commission either interesting or worthwhile? The answer lies with the ambivalent conception of the regulatory process that has become dominant among the American public today. On the one hand, the regulatory process is viewed as the only institutional guardian of the public interest, especially in areas of energy production and distribution. On the other, there is a growing distrust of the whole regulatory process, and a general suspicion that it is not serving the public interest as well as the public has a right to expect.

On the one hand, that is to say, consumers have come to think of the various regulatory commissions, state and federal, as their only "official" protection against self-serving financial manipulations on the part of the "energy establishment" in times of increasingly severe energy shortages. On the other, automatic "fuel cost adjustment" escalations and frequent increases in regular rates so common across the country today encourage the impression that the commissions often give the interests of the regulated industries priority over those of the public at large.

1

How do values come into the picture? One answer is the commonplace observation that the priorities of a commission are part of the values with which they operate, and that given our ambivalent popular understanding of the regulatory commissions these values are worth studying in themselves. But there is a more theoretical answer as well, having to do with our scholarly understanding of the regulatory process.

In the first chapter below we look at several standard economic and political theories of how the regulatory process actually works. Each of these academic theories, despite major differences in other respects, is critical of the so-called "Conventional Theory" by which regulation of industries "affected with a public interest" traditionally has been justified. According to the Conventional Theory, the purpose of regulation is to allow the public to share the savings resulting from noncompetitive provision of essential goods and services while at the same time protecting the public from the excessive fees for these goods and services that can develop when monopoly goes unchecked. In brief, regulation is supposed to provide to the public the advantages of being served by monopolistic enterprises without the usual disadvantages. The regulatory commissions make this possible by maintaining an independent check over both rates and profits of the regulated enterprises, thereby protecting the interests of the public at large.

According to the standard academic theories, by contrast, there are forces at work in the regulatory process that make it practically inevitable that a given regulatory commission will eventually be "captured" by the industry it is supposed to regulate, thus losing its capacity to serve as an independent representative of the public interest. The academic theories differ in their accounts of how this "capture" comes about. But all agree that the regulatory process tends eventually to come under the control of the industry it is supposed to regulate, and thus ultimately fails its intended purpose.

If the academic theories are right, there is no cause for wonder in the widespread suspicion that regulation in this country today is not serving the public interest as well as it should. And there is

an obvious explanation for the fact that the most vigorous defenders of regulation in its current form are
often the regulated industries themselves.

We believe, however, that there is an important
factor operating in the regulatory process which the
academic theories have left out of account. This factor is the value-orientation of the regulatory commission as a body, which in some way is a product of the
value-orientations of the individual regulators. In
ignoring this factor, the academic theories overlook
a major influence upon the capacity of a commission to
fulfill its intended role.

If the individual members of a given regulatory
body are guided by goals and standards giving priority to social and environmental concerns over concerns of the regulated industry, then it would seem
that the regulators as a group should remain able to
serve as effective representatives of the public interest despite other influences on their behavior.
However, if key members of a commission come to place
higher value upon the interests of the regulated industry, the regulatory process can easily be distort-
ed to serve the purposes of that sector as well. The
role of values within the regulatory process thus becomes a crucial issue not only for evaluating the adequacy of the standard academic theories of regulation,
but also for assessing the capacity of regulatory bodies as currently constituted to serve the purpose for
which they were intended.

The response of an academic theoretician to these
remarks would be that whatever values a commissioner
or key staff member might carry onto the job initially, the system of rewards and punishment operating
within the regulatory environment will eventually lead
to cooptation by the regulated industry. This claim,
however, has remained unsupported by empirical data.
To the contrary, empirical evidence has been found
during the present study which suggests that "capture"
by the industry is not as inevitable as the academic
theories maintain. If it can be shown that such "capture" is not inevitable, and that the public-oriented
values of the individual commissioners make a difference not only at the beginning but throughout their
careers, then an important flaw will have been disclosed in traditional theory of regulation. A con-

sequence which makes this possible flaw worth inves-
tigating is that the regulatory process as currently
functioning--given certain conditions regarding the
value-orientations of the regulators--may be a more
effective means than we have been led to expect of
protecting the consumer in monopolistic enterprises
"affected with a public interest."

The second chapter below describes the methodology of our empirical approach. One notable aspect of
this approach is that we have elected to confine the
study to the operations of a single state commission
in the regulation of electric power production and
delivery. The rationale for this limitation comes in
several parts. First, in order to arrive at an empirical answer to the question whether the value-orientations of particular individuals on a regulatory commission can influence the results of the regulatory
process itself, it is necessary to identify the specific values of individuals on a specific commission and
to correlate these values with dominant aspects of
their decision-making behavior. Although it would be
highly desirable to extend the study to regulation of
other industries, in other states, and on the national
level as well, there is no other way to begin than
with a detailed examination of a particular commission.

Second, a study comparable to the present one
has already been completed of the value-orientation
of a large electric power company in the Chicago area.
Choice of the Illinois Commerce Commission as subject
thus enables us to draw upon previously acquired information for a fuller understanding of the interaction between regulators and regulated industry. The
availability of data from this previous study also
dictates choice of electric power regulation as our
particular focus.

Other considerations recommending concentration
upon the Illinois Commerce Commission (ICC)* are the

*This acronym was chosen for brevity, despite the
possibility of confusion with the Interstate Commerce
Commission. The acronym employed for the latter (in
a title cited in Chapter Two) is 'I.C.C.'.

facts (i) that enabling legislation during earlier days of this commission served as a model for legislation in other states, and (ii) that the ICC enjoys a high reputation for professional ethics and for active concern with the public interest.

If the academic theories of regulation are right, then individual regulators tend eventually to come under the sway of the industries they regulate. If our conjecture that the value-orientations of individuals make a difference is right, on the other hand, we should expect to find an appreciable number even among veteran regulators in the ICC who are not "captured" by industry in this fashion. Our conjecture in this case would be that the value-orientations of regulators who are "captured" are different from those of regulators who are not, and that this difference in value-orientations would tell us something about the difference in relationship to the regulated industries.

Chapter Three, accordingly, addresses the hypothesis that a significant number of regulators within the ICC will be found not to be aligned with industry in any of the forms specified in the academic literature. A major finding stemming from our efforts to measure "capture" in these various forms is that some forms have to do with the structure of the regulatory process itself, while others are more a matter of individual discretion. A relatively trivial consequence of our data was that most regulators within the ICC are "captured" in respects that are unavoidable for structural reasons. Limiting our concern to individual forms of "capture" which are more discretional in character, and in which values therefore may be expected to make a difference, the result was that a majority of our respondents turn out not to be "captured."

Chapter Four explores the correlation between individual value-orientations, as disclosed by standard value tests, and degree of alignment with industry on the part of individual regulators. Data pertaining to this correlation are marshalled with respect to the hypothesis that aligned and nonaligned regulators will be characterized by different value-orientations, as measured by these standard tests. Results under this heading were ambiguous. Suffice

it to say by way of anticipation that we did not find
the general differences in value profile that had been
expected. As a consequence it became pertinent to focus upon a set of particular values that are directly
germane to the concerns of this study--those values
informing the regulators' conception of the public interest. A more specific hypothesis is that aligned
and nonaligned regulators will be found to subscribe
to different conceptions of the public interest. The
first part of Chapter Five evaluates empirical data
bearing on this more specific hypothesis.

To describe the value-orientations influencing
the decision-making of the regulatory body is essentially an empirical task. Of quite a different sort
is the task of evaluating these value-orientations
themselves. That a certain group of persons operates
with a certain set of values is simply a matter of
fact. But such a fact in itself might turn out to be
either good or bad. It would be good if the values
were morally commendable, and bad if they were deserving of moral censure. The study of what is deserving
of moral commendation and censure is known as ethical
theory, a discipline which has been cultivated by philosophers for at least twenty-five centuries. Despite
the longevity of the discipline, philosophers have not
been able to agree on issues of moral right and wrong.
What they have been able to agree on, however, is the
identity of a small number of specific theories about
what is morally good and bad, and the strengths and
weaknesses of these particular theories. This is very
helpful for purposes of the present study.

Rather than attempt to assess the value-orientation of the Commission as being either good or bad in
some categorical fashion, our approach at evaluation
has been to determine which of the specific moral theories generally recognized by philosophers comes closest to representing the dominant characteristics of
those value-orientations in question. This approach
allows us to reach conditional conclusions of the following form: insofar as the values of the Commission
are characterizable by such and such moral theory, and
insofar as this theory exhibits certain strengths and
weaknesses, then the values of the Commission may be
expected to exhibit the same strengths and weaknesses.
Moral theory thus provides a means for critique of the
Commission's values, without leading to categorical

moral judgments unsupported by data. These matters are treated in Chapter Six.

Chapter Seven, finally, draws consequences of our empirical and theoretical findings for the academic theories of regulation, and focuses the results of our ethical analysis upon a few possible problem areas upon which the Commission might want to reflect to increase its self-understanding.

Our thanks is due the Illinois Commerce Commission for their trust and cooperation, particularly to previous Chairman Marvin Lieberman whose encouragement was essential at the outset of the study. Thanks is due also those members of the project whose names are not included among those of the authors, but who contributed substantially to the contents of this volume: Mr. Matt Farner, Mr. Joseph DesJardins, and Sr. Mary Treanor. We are grateful to the National Science Foundation for support of this study under grant 00SS77-00984.

Any opinions, findings, and conclusions or recommendations expressed in this publication are those of the authors, and do not necessarily reflect the views of the National Science Foundation.

1 Theories of Regulation and the Dangers of Capture

THE CONVENTIONAL THEORY OF REGULATION

Public utility regulation as we know it began with the so-called Granger legislation. In the late 19th Century the agricultural states of the Midwest and the West attempted to regulate the railroads and grain elevators on which their access to Eastern markets depended. These statutes did not endure intact. However their pattern of government involvement in business through regulatory commissions was copied and became a permanent fixture of the American economy by the end of the century.

A series of Supreme Court cases, beginning with Munn v. Illinois (1877), established that if a business had a sufficient impact on the community, or a sufficient tendency to monopoly, then state or federal government could regulate it or empower a commission to do so. In its early form, regulation included: (a) limiting rates to what was required to generate a reasonable profit, (b) assigning territories or otherwise restricting entry into the regulated business so as to protect the investment of those already serving, and (c) setting terms of service to insure availability to all applicants on equal terms.

Illinois had been a pioneer in the establishment of regulatory commissions. The Railroad and Warehouse

Commission was set up by legislation in 1871, and figured in the landmark Munn v. Illinois decision. Although the governing statute of this commission has been amended from time to time, and its name and organization have been altered, both statute and organization were typical of present commissions.

A century of experience and precedents shaped an account of economic regulation which is generally accepted as its official justification in the United States. This account, referred to as the "Conventional Theory of Regulation," describes the conditions under which and purposes for which an enterprise should be regulated and justifies the independent regulatory commission as the proper agent of regulation.

According to the Conventional Theory, the purpose of regulation derives from two coequal principles. One is that some business activities are especially "affected with the public interest," and thus should be guided by public and not private decisions. The second is that the regulated business enterprise is constitutionally guaranteed that its property will not be taken "without just compensation." Regulation thus is conceived to balance public claims upon private property against the rights of due process attached to that property. The history of the Conventional Theory involves a struggle to clarify these principles and to resolve the tensions between them.

A business enterprise "affected with the public interest" has that status either because of the peculiar value given its services at a specific place and time or because it requires monopolistic status to perform those services efficiently. The determination whether an enterprise is so "affected," and hence constitutes a public utility appropriate for regulation, depends upon the level of public concern for that enterprise's service. As Mr. Justice Brandeis observed:

> The public's concern about a particular
> business may be so pervasive and varied
> as to require...a very high degree of
> regulation....It is to such businesses
> that the designation 'public utility' is
> commonly applied (New State Ice Co. v.
> Liebmann).

Over the past hundred years, for example, not only railroads and granaries, but also slaughterhouses, bus lines, parking facilities, towing companies, trash haulers, and not least electric power companies, have been objects of such public concern.

While monopolistic organization of an industry is not essential for designation as a public utility (trash hauling and interstate trucking, for example, are "affected with a public interest" but are not monopolistic), the existence of a "natural monopoly" amounts to a prima facie case for the designation. Characteristically, a "natural monopoly" is a public utility because its requirements for doing business strip away the "natural" protections for the public provided by a competitive market.

The primary purpose of regulation, according to the Conventional Theory, is to provide maximum benefits to society from these "natural monopolies" and other enterprises "affected with a public interest," while preventing them from charging higher prices than the competitive market would allow. In effect, regulation is viewed as simulating the effects of the competitive market for publicly important enterprises that function best in the absence of competition.

While regulation attempts to simulate the effects of the marketplace for the public advantage, a result is that the regulated firm is left without the freedom to remove its product from the marketplace when profits diminish. Since it is compelled by law to provide its service at a controlled rate, the firm also requires protection of its economic interests. How is the rate charged for its services to be calculated so as to protect both the public and the firm? The answer to this question has been subject of debate through a large part of the history of regulation. For the first four decades of the 20th century, the Supreme Court's decision in Smyth v. Ames (1898) provided the generally accepted solution to the problem. The court held that a regulated rate must follow a "fair value" rule. To be fair to the firm, its rate base should be assessed at the "cost of replacement" of land, equipment, and other facilities.

While Smyth v. Ames served as precedent in rate cases through the 1930's, there was a stream of criti-

cism charging that this precedent tended to maximize
the profits of regulated firms by allowing them the
most extensive basis for calculating capital worth.
Mr. Justice Brandeis was the leading critic of this
precedent and its "fair value" rule. In a series of
dissenting opinions, Justice Brandeis argued that
the rate base ought to constitute the dollar amount
originally invested in the firm's equity securities.

In Federal Power Commission v. Hope Natural Gas
(1944), the Court abandoned the specificity of Smyth
v. Ames and explicitly recognized the acceptability
of standards for the calculation of rate base other
than "replacement cost." The Hope case allowed the
commissions of the federal government and of the individual states to choose the basis upon which proper
return would be calculated. In effect, the Court was
recognizing the constitutionality of Justice Brandeis'
"original cost" standard. The key to the Court's decision in Hope is its notion of "prudent investment"
as a guide to what constitutes a proper return on
capital investment. As Mr. Justice Douglas stated in
the majority opinion: "Rates which enable the company to operate successfully...to attract capital, and
to compensate investors for the risk assumed cannot
be considered invalid, even though they might produce
only a meager return on the so-called 'fair value'
rate base." In the wake of this decision, rate base
calculation became a statutory and policy concern of
the individual regulatory agencies. Although the constitutional protection of a business enterprise from
removal of its property "without just compensation"
guarantees it access to the courts for relief from improper rates, the role of the courts in determining
rates receded.

Throughout this debate, the Conventional Theory
remained clear in its principle that regulation should
be in the hands of independent regulatory commissions.
The emphasis here upon independence highlights the
single most important operating assumption of the Conventional Theory. While this theory admits that the
initial decision whether a given industry should be
regulated is largely prudential, it assumes that once
the decision is made the regulatory process itself can
proceed on an entirely objective basis. The Conventional Theory assumes that specific guidelines can be
abstracted from the free market in operation and ap-

11

plied to regulated enterprises in an objective calculus, thus arriving at proper rate structures which
yield returns equivalent to those which would develop
in a fully competitive market.

But if regulation is to produce results which
approximate those of the free market, then its mechanisms must be designed to be protected from influences that might distort this process, such as the
influences of the political system. Indeed the origin of regulation in the Granger movement bespeaks
its traditionally anti-political orientation, backed
up by the notion that reform of the political system
can be accomplished only by removing it from the control of the politicians (McConnell, 1966, p.43).

Emphasis upon independence in the early regulatory environment also had a practical justification.
As more enterprises became recognized as public utilities in the early 20th Century, and as rate calcula-
tions became increasingly complex, legislatures came
to view the commissions they created as specialists
in determining rate levels equivalent to those a competitive market would produce. Regulation came to
be considered a technical exercise which legislatures
could delegate to the commissions, but one to which
the political process itself could make no competent
contribution. Thus the practical requirements of
technical expertise reinforced the traditional anti-
political ideology of the regulatory process.

Independence from legislature, executive, and
judiciary freed the regulatory commissions from the
limits and checks which characterize American constitutional government. In fact, while the commissions
were substantially isolated from the major branches
of government they combined the functions of these
other branches. They were legislative in that they
made rules of general applicability to govern regulated enterprises. They were executive in that they
implemented these rules as well as their governing
statutes. And they were judicial in that they acted
on evidence after airing the positions of effected
parties in quasi-judicial hearings, and their specific orders applied the law to individual cases.

This hybrid status encouraged confusion over
whom or what the regulatory commissions were meant

12

to serve. The assumption of the Conventional Theory that the regulatory process should duplicate the effects of a free market carries with it the assumption that regulation is for the protection of the public, since the free market in the context of this theory is viewed as yielding outcomes in conformity with the public interest (Barnes, 1942, 282-283, Bonbright, 1961, 48-62). At the same time, however, there was a tendency in the 19th and the first decades of the 20th Centuries to see the law generally as a kind of neutral arbitrator among competing private interests. The public interest accordingly was sometimes seen as an additional competitor, rather than as a limit to the whole competitive system or as a matrix within which competition took place. On this understanding of the public interest, the regulatory commission was conceived as playing a neutral role rather than as vindicating the public interest per se.

Whereas the thinking that produced the commissions in the first place had conceived them precisely as advocates of the public interest, regulated industry came to view them as judicial boards upon which it could rely for assurance of fair rates and profits. In this view, for the commission to side actively with the public was for them to abdicate the function of impartial judges. As Samuel Insull (1924, p. 63) put it, a

> quite serious trouble is that a great many of the commissions, especially the newly created ones, think their function is to persecute or prosecute public utilities and that they are merely the advocates or protectors of the public, and not the judges between the public and the utilities.

This ambiguity regarding the allegiances and role of the regulatory commissions continues to the present. On the one hand, the Conventional Theory providing official justification of the regulatory process stresses the role of protecting the public interest against the abuses of monopoly. On the other hand, the day-to-day practice of regulation exerts a considerable pressure upon the regulators to adopt the viewpoints of the regulated industries. This continuing clash between rationale and practice has led to extensive criticism of the Conventional Theory.

13

THE CONVENTIONAL THEORY TODAY

Of the major industrial nations of the world today, the United States retains the greatest commitment to capitalism. Whereas the European democracies typically deal with enterprises "affected with a public interest" by assigning them to government-owned corporations, our characteristic method has been to rely on private industry regulated by independent commissions. But the theory by which this method is justified is in a state of crisis.

The crisis of the Conventional Theory has two separate strands. First, grave doubts have arisen over the theory of organization built into the Conventional Theory, particularly with regard to the justification of the independent regulatory commission. Second, the application to specific industries of the Conventional Theory's conception of public utility and "natural monopoly" has been treated with withering criticism (e.g., Schwartz, 1959; Kohlmeier, 1969; Krasnow and Longley, 1973).

Reformers have attacked the commissions as inefficient, incapable, and corrupt. Instead of the original model of the commissions as independent and neutral instruments of a calculus of regulation, the critics argue that they are understaffed and underbudgeted agencies led by commissioners who are often the dregs of the political patronage system.

An even more striking charge is that the commissions, instead of serving the public interest, are loyal agents of the industries they regulate. Critics point to the frequent protectiveness of commissions over industries, and the commitment of commissions to maintain price structures against competitive undercutting. Suggesting sordid political pressure and corruption, these critics charge that in some undefined way the commissions are captives of the industries they are supposed to regulate.

Furthermore, some critics ask, what beyond tradition endows one industry with concerns of a public interest and not another? Why, for instance, do we regulate interstate trucking and not the interstate manufacture of automobiles? Or, as Louis Kohlmeier asks (Kohlmeier, 1969, Ch. 7), why do we regulate

14

through independent commissions a number of industries
with highly competitive internal structures, while we
leave oligopolies like automobile manufacturing, alu-
minum, petroleum, and steel untouched?

Until recently regulation of the electric power
industry by state commissions has escaped the criticism to which other independent regulatory commissions
have been subjected. This area seemed to present the
model case of good regulation. If any industry could
claim to be a "natural" monopoly it must be electricity. Moreover, as opposed to the common appearance
of regulation stabilizing high prices against competition in other industries, across the nation the retail price of electricity went up only 12 percent from
1947 to 1967 while the consumer price index climbed 50
percent (Ford Foundation, 1974, p. 255).

By the late 1960's, however, the retail price of
electricity began to increase. After the sudden rise
of fuel prices in 1973, the cost of electricity itself
zoomed upward. As a result, the electric power industry and its regulators no longer could remain exempt
from criticism. The energy crisis suddenly made the
general critique of the conventional theory of regulation apply dramatically to regulation of this industry in particular. With increasingly higher rate
schedules, the formerly quiet rate hearings by state
public service commissions became battlegrounds on
which power companies faced irate customers.

This new regulatory climate placed new demands
upon the state regulatory commissions. For one thing,
consumers demanded that the commissions deny company
requests for rate increases and for automatic fuel
cost surcharges. For another, state regulators were
called upon for the first time to do more than merely
to oversee the efficient distribution of power at
free-market prices. Public interest groups now demanded
that the regulators discourage the expansion of generating facilities, that they take greater cognizance
of the environmental impacts, and that they restruc-
ture a rate system originally meant to encourage the
use of electricity so as to remove those incentives
or even outrightly to discourage such use.

In brief, the state independent regulatory commissions have been thrust from a stable regulatory

environment, within which decision-making was wholly
incremental and the most important function was protection against discriminatory rates, into a new
environment in which all the formerly routine assumptions and practices of electric power regulation are
thrown into question. The implicit mandate of the
commissions in the former regulatory environment was
to encourage the expansion of energy use. That public
mandate has ended and the public now demands that the
regulatory commissions develop radically different
policies to guide the electric power industry. It remains to be seen whether the state commissions are
capable of responding adequately to this new environment and these new demands.

Current discussion of regulation suggests that
the Conventional Theory remains alive in the face of
crisis. The very fact that new demands arising from
a changed regulatory environment are directed to the
commissions suggests that the public expects the commissions to reform both themselves and the industries
they regulate. New concerns about regulation have
not led to a widespread call for abandonment of the
state regulatory commissions. Academic literature on
regulation, however, warns that the independent regulatory commission may be incapable of significant
change. In sharp contrast to the Conventional Theory,
academic thinking on the topic bespeaks considerable
pessimism about regulation by independent commissions.

Consideration of the character and claims of the
academic literature on regulation is an important step
in addressing the possibilities of policy change in
the regulation of electric power. The regulation of
the electric power industry takes place primarily on
the state level and predominantly through independent
commissions. We cannot blithely assume that these
state commissions possess the capacity to develop
policy innovations to meet the new energy climate of
the 1970's and beyond. As a necessary step in the
current discussion over energy-policy planning in this
country, we must assess the capacity of the independent regulatory commission to generate policy in response to public needs instead of to the interests of
the regulated industry.

What help towards clarifying the character of
independent regulatory commissions can be gained from

16

the scholarly literature on regulation? While the
writing on regulation has focused primarily on federal commissions, it tends to assume that all commissions contend with the same forces, no matter what
industry they regulate or at what level of government
they serve. Further, state governments are based on
the same separation-of-powers model as is the federal
government. Hence it is sensible to assume that the
theories represented in this literature can be gen-
eralized.

Three different fields--political science, law,
and economics--have contributed to our understanding
of regulation. These fields bring different perspectives, techniques, and levels of analysis to bear upon
the subject. But they all lead to the same striking
result. For differing reasons, they all lead us to
see the regulatory commission as subject to "capture"
by its clients. In the words of Warren J. Samuels
(Samuels, 1972, p. 9), an institutional economist,
while "it is conventional to perceive utilities and
regulatory commissions as separate and distinct, albeit interacting, entities . . . both should be seen
primarily as part of the holistic, complex and dy-
namically changing structure of power, opportunity
sets, and exercise of mutual coercion that is the
public utility decision process." Samuels' insistence
upon viewing the regulator-regulated relationship as
one system of management decisions is an explicit
statement of what is implicit in all the academic theories of regulation.

Academic theories of regulation are, in effect,
theories of "capture." But they vary in their identification of the causes of "capture." We will examine a number of these theories, organizing our
analysis on the basis of whether a theory identifies
the prime variable leading to "capture" as 1) structure, 2) policy, or 3) characteristic behavior of the
individual regulator.

STRUCTURAL ACCOUNTS OF REGULATION

A structural theory of regulation, as understood
here, is one that identifies the organization of a
regulatory commission as the independent variable in
accounting for its behavior. Two prominent theories

of regulation fall within this category. One we shall
call the "executive branch" theory, the other the
"life cycle" theory.

The general thrust of the "executive branch" theory is that regulatory commissions malfunction because
they violate the concept of separation of powers.
Proponents of this theory advocate[1] that the work of
the commissions be integrated more closely with other
executive branch functions.

In 1937 the President's Committee on Administrative Management (President's Committee, 1937) charged
that the independent regulatory commissions constituted "a headless fourth branch of government," performing crucial tasks in guiding the American economy,
yet lying beyond the chief executive's immediate capacity to affect their decisions, to integrate their
activities with executive branch policies, or to oversee their managerial functions or choice of priorities
for future investigations and activities. In short,
the commissions were powerful but unguided.

The Committee believed that good management was
democracy's handmaiden, and that the chief executive
was this country's guarantee of stable democracy.
Thus an organization of government which stymied the
chief executive, and reduced his capacity to innovate,
to coordinate, and to control policy and its implementation, was counterproductive. The President's Committee recommended increased executive control over
the regulatory commissions.

This recommendation was to be implemented in two
steps. First, the commissions should be integrated
with the line departments of the executive branch,
but care must be taken to place them in agencies which
are "neutral" with regard to the regulated industry.
Second, the functions of the new regulatory agencies
should be divided between those which are executive
and those which involve judicial elements. Executive
functions belong within the executive branch of government, while judicial functions should operate separately from the executive activities as do the administrative law judges in many line agencies. Thus,
even while the President's Committee attacked the organizational status of the commission form, in the end it
accepted part of the rationale for their original in-

dependence--the necessity of impartiality in the adjudicative functions of the commission.

The next noteworthy expression of the "executive branch" theory came with an accompanying task force report to the first Hoover Commission, a major reorganization planning effort in 1949. This Commission created numerous research task forces to investigate particular problems. The task force on regulation noted that commissions were not fulfilling their intended functions. Commission members were not particularly strong or interested people, and they were not adequately prepared for their jobs. Their staffs were not properly coordinated and the administrative work of the commissions generally was ineffective. There was no central planning and coordinating within the commissions. Further, there was no system of planning which tied together the commissions and the executive branch (U.S. Commission, 1948).

The Hoover Commission task force's recommendations echoed those of the President's Committee in that it agreed that no commission should possess independent executive functions. Rather than boldly recommending that such functions be merged back into the executive branch, however, the task force expressed the opinion that the means existed, particularly with the practice of the President designating the chairman, for the chief executive to provide general guidance to the commissions.

Both of these reports identified the causes of the regulatory commissions' failures in their structural weaknesses. The President's Committee asserted that the commissions' independence from the President removed them from effective leadership and policy coordination, and it assumed that merging the commissions into the executive branch would provide those missing qualities for more successful operation. The task force of the Hoover Commission, on the other hand, saw the problems of the commissions as largely internal, due to structure ill-suited for administrative efficacy. Its recommendations for dealing with the problem involved the presidential designation of a chairman and the reorganization of staff functions around the chairman, who now became the administrative head of the commission. But, for the task force, the independence of the commissions remained impor-

tant. Far more than the President's Committee, it
reflected an acceptance of elements of the Conventional Theory. Nevertheless, the task force admitted
that presidential leadership was important and asserted that it was possible within the existing system.

The "executive branch" theory was an expression
of the strong pro-executive movement which affected
students of American government after 1930. The
Presidency and the gubernatorial offices of the states
were held out as offering the answers to a variety of
public and governmental problems, if only they were
freed of their historical weaknesses. If the executive could be strengthened, it was thought, it would
become the preeminent political institution for artic-
ulating the public interest and asserting accountabil-
ity in government.

A more recent proponent of this view is Robert G.
Dixon, former Assistant Attorney General and presently
professor at the George Washington University Law Center. Dixon has forwarded a sophisticated version of
the executive branch theory which contains elements of
the "life cycle" theory that we examine next (Dixon,
1975). He observes that the independence of the regulatory commissions puts them beyond the mechanisms of
the popular political process through which major
choices are made for society. This independence is
most defensible, he argues, where the operations of an
agency are highly formalized and wholly adjudicatory.
But, in the case of agencies where many of the actual
decisions arise from informal negotiations and where
the major work of the agency is policy making, independence is indefensible precisely because it precludes popular participation in decision-making.
Finally, Dixon also notes (Dixon, 1975, p. 16) that
early in the life of a commission it probably does not
matter that it is independent since at that point it
is still motivated by the popular political pressure
which led to its creation.

It is only in successive administrations
that independence problem arises. From
this standpoint, the independent commission
is a device whereby the agitated partisan
of the present--and they may be very good
partisans with very contemporary ideas--may

put shackles on the agitated partisans
of the future who will face different
problems and have different priorities.

This brings us to the second sort of structural
account of the independent commissions, the "life cycle" theory of regulation. This theory is more satisfactory than the first in that it offers an explanation for a larger portion of the observable behavior
of the commissions. The "life cycle" theory is an attempt to offer structural reasons for the early vigor
and later decline of the regulatory commissions.

A classic study implicating a "life cycle" theory
is Samuel Huntington's "The Marasmus of the I.C.C."
(Huntington, 1952). The Interstate Commerce Commission, the first of the federal independent regulatory
commissions, worked with some distinction in its early
years. But, Huntington noted, by the late 1930's the
agency seemed tired, haggard, and even irrelevant to
the central thrust of transportation policy at the
federal level.

In Huntington's view, the Interstate Commerce
Commission spent the first three decades of its life
attempting to police the railroad industry. From its
creation in 1887 to the early years of the new century
it fought a losing battle against the railroads and
the courts to maintain stringent regulation in the
industry. In 1906 Congress reinvigorated the commission with the Hepburn Act, broadening its powers over
tariffs and regulation of freight. The following decade saw the Commission reach the zenith of its power
and prestige.

The Transportation Act of 1920 again broadened
the responsibilities and mission of the Commission.
This act is often cited by students of regulation as
a keystone in the change in spirit and intent of regulation by independent commission. Now regulation
was to be benign. The Interstate Commerce Commission
was to fix rates which would earn a "fair return upon
the aggregate value" of a company's capital. The act
specified also that the Commission would now have
power to permit pooling of service by companies, to
draw up plans of consolidation creating smaller numbers of larger systems, and to allow transfers of excess profits between companies. In a sense, the 1920

21

Act converted the regulators from policemen to cartel managers.

In light of these changes, Huntington argues that after 1920 the Interstate Commerce Commission became a partner of the regulated industry. The industry provided the Commission with its sole frame of reference. The Commission's purpose was to regulate and to protect. Huntington states (Huntington, 1952, p. 473): "The attitude of the railroads towards the Commission since 1935 can only be described as one of satisfaction, approbation, and confidence." Most telling is the fact that the regulated industry used all of its political influence to maintain the Commission's independence. The railroad industry opposed the reorganization of the Commission proposed in the President's reorganization plans of 1950. The leading element of these plans for the independent commissions was that the President would henceforth have the power to designate the chairmen of the commissions. The industry lobbied hard enough in Congress so that the Interstate Commerce Commission was the only commission exempted from this plan.

Furthermore, the industry has opposed the creation of any agency which would rival the Commission's role, fighting instead to expand the powers of the Commission to include rate regulation for interstate truck and barge traffic. Thus the railroad industry used the Interstate Commerce Commission as a partner to control competition from alternative modes of transportation.

As a result of this partnership, Huntington argues, the Commission was sidetracked from the ongoing development and change in American transportation policy. More important, the Commission lost its capability of regulating the railroads on the basis of a reasonable conception of the public interest.

What caused this decline over the life cycle of the Interstate Commerce Commission? Huntington observes (Huntington, 1952, p. 470):

> Successful adaptation to changing environmental circumstances is the secret of health and longevity for administrative agencies as well as biological organisms.

22

> Every governmental agency must reflect
> to some degree the 'felt needs' of its
> time . . . . Felt needs are expressed
> through political demands and political
> pressures. These . . . may come from
> the president, other administrative
> agencies and officials, congressmen,
> political interest groups, and the gen-
> eral public. If an agency is to be
> viable it must adapt itself to the pres-
> sure from these sources so as to main-
> tain a net preponderence of political
> support over political opposition . . . .
> If the agency fails to make this adjust-
> ment, its political support decreases
> relative to its political opposition,
> and it may be said to suffer from admin-
> istrative marasmus.

To react to changing circumstances, to reorganize
their priorities, and to respond to new political
demands, agencies must be accessible to a diverse
constituency. In terms of Huntington's biological
metaphor, an organism cannot survive if it cannot
sense its environment. Huntington argues that an
agency's capacity for healthy response and change
depends upon its links to the President, to other
agencies, to Congress, and to the public.

By design, however, independent commissions are
removed from the possibility of healthy response to
their political environment. Whereas in the Conventional Theory of independent commissions isolation
is a virtue, the practical result is that the commissions all too often end up with only one voice to
listen to, that of the regulated industry.

Huntington's account of regulation is structural
in conception because he identifies the failure of
the independent commission to respond to its changing
political environment as resulting from the vacuum
caused by its independence within the structure of
government. His theory thus amounts to an elabora-
tion of the basic structural view we find in the "executive branch" theory, in that he adds the life cycle
as another dimension of explanation. He observes
that the commissions begin with vigor because they
start with the support of a broad political coalition

23

in favor of regulation. When the initial political
fervor is gone, however, an older commission faces
the prospect of declining support, lessened visibility, and "capture."

Another political scientist, Marver Bernstein,
elaborated on this "life cycle" view of independent
commissions in arguing that all independent commissions follow a set pattern of development (Bernstein,
1955, p. 74):

> The life cycle of an independent commis-
> sion can be divided into four periods;
> gestation, youth, maturity, and old age.
> The length of each phase varies from one
> commission to another, and sometimes a
> whole period seems to be skipped. Some
> commissions maintain their youthfulness
> for a fairly long time, while others seem
> to age rapidly and apparently never pass
> through a period of optimistic adolescence.
> Some are adventurous while others are
> bound more closely to the pattern estab-
> lished by the oldest commission, the ICC.
> Such differences add an element of inter-
> est and reality to the evolution of com-
> mission regulation, but they do not
> invalidate generalizations about the ad-
> ministrative history of regulation.

Bernstein's "life cycle" account begins with
gestation. Regulation most frequently is a product
of long political struggle, and regulatory legislation is typically passed only after the "losing" side
has been able to win significant compromises. While
the regulatory commission is the product of a victo-
rious political movement, it contains political compromises.

The political forces which fought for years to
pass regulatory legislation become, upon passage of
that law, the supporting constituency behind the new
regulatory commission. They lobby the Congress and
the President for more powers and larger budgets for
"their" agency. They lobby the commission itself to
press forward on its regulatory mission with fervor.
At times these supporters turn on "their" agency with
the wrath of spurned lovers. The political coalition

24

which created regulatory legislation demands that the
instrument of regulation remain true to the goal of
the coalition.

After establishment, the independent commission
enters youth. In this period it probably will attempt to maintain its vitality and independence, but
will do so only with increasing difficulty. The most
important general development of this period, according to Bernstein, is the fading of high levels of
public concern with a particular regulatory arena.
Public attention is short-lived, and the routine practice of regulation is far less exciting than the original battle to pass regulatory legislation. Even the
politically astute citizen often assumes that the formation of public policy is set in the legislative process, and that administration simply involves the implementation of statutory directions. As the heat of
the legislative battle dissipates, many originally
interested parties redirect their interests to new
political causes. The old field of battle is left in
the shared possession of the regulatory agency and the
regulated industry.

Still young enough to be concerned with its mission, the agency finds itself on the defensive against
the regulated industry. The industry brings immense
resources to bear in its attempts to bend the regulatory process to its interests. For one thing, it
controls the sources of technical data upon which regulatory decisions are made. For another, the industry
can spend large amounts of tax-deductible funds to
hire first-class legal and technical talent to sway
and to contest decisions of the regulators. Finally,
the regulatory commissioners are personally threaten-
ed with cooptation by the industry through professional and social contact, job opportunities and so forth.
For these reasons, Bernstein suggests, the commission
concerned with maintaining its energy and independence
in its youth is fated to fight a losing battle.

The third phase of a commission's life is its
maturity. This is a period in which the agency has
achieved an equilibrium position within its political
environment. It becomes accepted as an essential
part of the industrial system and tries to prevent
changes which adversely affect the general health of
the industry (Bernstein, 1955, p. 87). The commis-

25

sion has been transformed from an agency in the midst of political struggle over the methods and goals of regulation, to an agency without political following and with little political visibility outside the regulated industry.

In its maturity, the independent regulatory commission in effect has become part of the regulated industry. The industry provides its major political support, while in turn the commission's authority becomes a crucial force in stabilizing the industry. The regulatory process thus remains alive as part of the dynamic system within which a major industry functions. But the goal of the original regulatory legislation is lost. The commission does not police the industry; it acts as a partner.

At this stage, the regulatory commission brings public authority to the industry as a device for stability. It sets prices or rates at levels which guarantee profits even to weak, inefficient firms. It closes off entry to the industry by newcomers, thereby creating an oligopoly for the existing firms. Through control of techniques by which products or services are delivered, it protects the industry from the dangers of technological innovation. Thus commission and industry become a closed system.

As the aging regulatory commission comes to be recognized as a "captive" of the regulated industry, the legislature and the public view it with increasing distrust. The legislature will not trust it with new grants of authority. Its budgets fail to grow at the pace of the average increase of the governmental budget. As Bernstein notes (Bernstein, 1955, p. 93), there arises "the fear that further additions to budget and staff will not make the agency more efficient and only commit it irrevocably to outworn procedures and policies."

According to Bernstein's account of the rise and fall of regulatory agencies, the final shame of the commission will come with the occurrence of a crisis relating to its regulatory mission. In the face of crisis, the executive and legislature will seek some policy through which to restore order in a crucial economic sector. Although there already exists an agency which has long experience with the industry,

26

the policy-making branches of the government likely
will look past the old commission and create a new
bureaucracy for implementing new policies created in
the face of crisis. Overtaken by a serious crisis
of this sort, the old commission will recede into the
background and lose additional budgetary support
(Bernstein, 1955, p. 93). Alternatively, the government may choose simply to abolish or radically to
reorganize the original agency. Only in the latter
case will new policy be placed in its care.

POLICY ACCOUNTS OF REGULATION

Policy accounts of regulation by independent
commission attribute the failure of the commissions
to the character of the policy they implement. These
accounts share the pessimistic view of regulation
found in the structural theories, but attribute the
failure of the system to the way it is understood.

The first policy-based account of regulation we
will examine views the independent commission as a
"missionless branch" of government. Both political
scientists and legal scholars have adopted this view.
They argue that to understand the character of the
regulatory commissions we must begin with the standards and guidelines initially imposed by empowering
statutes. These standards tend to be imprecise as a
result of the legislative process by which regulatory
statutes are created. For one thing, the statute
generally constitutes a treaty of compromise after a
long, heated political battle. An important aspect
of the compromise often is the postponement of a range
of important issues to be decided by the commission
rather than by the legislature. For another, the legislature, because of lack of time and expertise,
writes statutes that are vague in crucial aspects.

As a result, the legislature most often tells the
regulatory commission little more than to regulate in
the public interest and to keep the regulated industry
healthy. What guidelines does this provide for later
decisions of the regulatory commission? "Missionless
branch" proponents answer that such statutes provide
no guidelines at all, which is precisely the problem.

According to this view, two fundamental problems

27

arise from a lack of standards by which regulatory commissions can shape their policy as they move from case to case. First, the parties affected by the actions of the commission cannot predict the likely outcome of particular cases because the principles upon which each case will be decided are not evident in advance. Second, the commission, lacking purpose and clear direction, begins to drift under the influence of the regulated industry, which offers a clear and continuing sense of what it ought to be doing.

Adherents of the "missionless branch" account among legal scholars argue that the lack of clear standards is not merely a legislative failure, and in fact stems from no single source. As Judge Henry Friendly puts it (Friendly, 1962, p. 6):

> There have been failures . . . by Congress at the time of initial enactment, failures by the agencies to shape the vague contours of the original statute, failures by the legislature to supply more definite standards as growing experience has permitted or even demanded, and failures by the executive to spur the legislature into activity. All these failures have been interdependent: failure by the agency to make clear what it is doing impedes both executive challenge and legislative response.

Regardless of where the lack comes from, however, these scholars see the commissions themselves as the most likely source of consistent standards to make up the deficiency. In effect, they propose that a commission should guide itself into a position of greater clarity and predictability of behavior. Professor Kenneth Davis has argued that courts must demand that agencies formalize and broadcast their methods, processes, and policies (Davis, 1969, p. 50). "The hope lies," he thinks, "not in better statutory standards, but in earlier and more elaborate administrative rule-making and in better structuring and checking of discretionary power."

What benefits would flow from clear standards and predictable actions in the regulatory process? Judge Friendly answers by stating the central thesis of the

"missionless branch" theory. The importance of the
development of standards in the regulatory process is
that

> this is necessary to the maintenance of
> the independence which the agencies so
> highly prize. The revulsion against the
> revelations of pressure on the commission
> from businessmen, legislators, and the
> executive branch has been too much con-
> cerned with the symptom and too little
> with the cause . . . . Lack of definite
> standards creates a void into which
> attempts to influence are bound to rush;
> legal vacuums are quite like physical
> vacuums in that respect (Friendly, 1962,
> p. 22).

While the soothing, affirmative language legislators
write into the organic statutes of regulatory commissions offers the public a positive sense of government at work in their interest, at the very same
time the vague language of these statutes helps
create a milieu conducive to "capture."

Another set of policy-based accounts of the regulatory process is offered within the discipline of
economics. Unlike political scientists and lawyers,
who focus heavily on the organization and process of
regulation generally, economists have given extended
attention to the particular phenomenon of the regulation of electric power companies. From an economic
perspective this particular area of regulation is an
ideal subject for study, representing as it does one
of the clearest cases of price regulation over a dis-
crete and measurable commodity.

For our purposes, economists who are students of
regulation may be divided into two schools. One is
the institutionalist school which, decades ago, contributed the major elements of what we have called the
"Conventional Theory" of regulation. Today, this same
school often offers critiques of regulation which are
akin to the theories of the political scientists which
we have already reviewed. The other major school is
the neoclassical. Its approach to regulation is
through the application of exchange models derived
from classical economic theory of the market.

Two major neoclassical contributions to regulatory theory are the Averch-Johnson model of electric power regulation and the work of the so-called "Chicago School." Both of these theoretical contributions are policy-based in the sense that they locate the causes for the ostensible weaknesses of regulation in the character and goals of regulatory policy. Averch and Johnson (1962) postulate that regulatory policy which allows a specific profitability above the cost of doing business (which prevails in most states) enables the firm to earn a higher return on capital investment than the cost of obtaining that capital. Given certain assumptions, they show that the regulated firm will use more capital than would be dictated by considerations of cost minimization. In effect, regulation of rate-of-return allegedly causes inefficient production through the overuse of capital, because the firm can increase its profits merely by increasing its capital investment.

There have been many refinements to the basic Averch-Johnson formulation. Given the wide variety of possible theoretical outcomes that can be deduced from an Averch-Johnson model, the question arises whether there is empirical evidence that these models provide any useful insights for the delineation of regulatory alternatives. What little empirical testing has been done seems to lend support to the Averch-Johnson thesis (Petersen, 1975; Sheshinski, 1971; Spann, 1974). This suggests, as a practical outcome, that the technical formula on which regulation rests abets "capture," in the sense that it leads agencies to support capital investment patterns in the electric power industry which stem from profitability motives rather than motives of efficiency.

Adherents of the Chicago School offer a less technical account of the regulatory process. We observe the emergence of the modern Chicago school approach to regulation in Milton Friedman's Capitalism and Freedom (1962), in which he argues for unregulated private monopolies. Professor Friedman and his followers maintain that regulation distorts the natural workings of the market and creates the worst kind of monopoly, because it links public authority with economic power. The unregulated monopoly, on the other hand, is less stable than the regulated monopoly and more likely to be responsive to changes in market demand and threats of competition.

From the standpoint of the neoclassical economist, the effectiveness of regulation in promoting the public interest is measured by Pareto optimality. A Pareto optimal situation is one where it is impossible to alter the allocation of resources so as to make anyone better off without worsening the situation of at least one person. Alternative allocations thus can be evaluated by asking whether it is possible to compensate losers so that they are no worse off than before while allowing some of the advantages which would accrue to the gainers to be retained. If the answer is affirmative, then such a reorganization of benefits is in the public interest. This outcome is most likely in an economy characterized by perfect competition. Monopoly distorts the optimum allocation of goods by limiting output below that which would be forthcoming from a perfectly competitive industry. Regulation is effective, then, to the extent that the monopolist is forced to produce a quantity of output approximating that of a competitive industry with the result that prices will also approximate those charged by a competitive firm. Thus the neoclassical economist uses Pareto optimality to undergird a perception of regulation very close to the ideals of the Conventional Theory described above.

THEORIES BASED ON INDIVIDUAL BEHAVIOR

A third group of theories about the regulatory process see the problem of regulation as one of pressures on individual regulators. In these theories the failures of regulation lie not so much in organizational or policy characteristics of the commissions themselves as in the character, motivation and resulting behavior of the individuals staffing them.

Three theories regarding individual behavior frequently appear in the literature of regulation. We will treat them in order of increasing complexity. All three theories have a common theme. They agree that the behavior of the regulators is geared to the expectations and desires of the regulated industry.

The simplest theory is what we shall call the "muckraking account" of regulation. It accounts for failures of regulation simply in terms of self-serving and often corrupt actions by the regulator. The assumption here is that the individual regulator serves time in his or her public position until given an opportunity to join the regulated industry, presumably at a far higher salary than available in the public role. In its most strident form, for example in some journalistic critiques of regulatory agencies, the "muckraking account" amounts to little more than an assertion of the rampant corruption of appointees to the regulatory commissions.

At a more scholarly level some researchers have used variations of the "muckraking account" to indicate a complicity between regulated and regulator. For example, in his work on governmental regulatory decisions regarding the oil industry, Professor Robert Engler observes that the long term personal interests of those who make public decisions concerning oil are identical with the interests of the oilmen, because they are virtually the same people in different roles. He argues that service on governmental commissions is a rotating door through which this industry places and then rehires its own (Engler, 1961).

Other studies of the relationship between regulated industries and regulators offer conclusions similar to Engler's findings. In a study of prestigious Washington law firms representing regulated industry Joseph Goulden states (Goulden, 1972, p. 6):

> Relations between some . . . lawyers and
> officials in the regulatory agencies can
> be so intimate they embarrass an onlooker.
> The lawyers and the regulators work to-
> gether in a tight, impenetrable community
> where an outsider can't understand the
> language, much less why things are done
> the way they are. The lawyers and regu-
> lators play together . . . . They fre-
> quently swap jobs, the regulator moving
> to the private bar, the Washington lawyer
> moving into the Commission on a "public
> service" leave of absence from his firm.

Goulden finds that the most common movement between regulated and regulator is not directly between industry and commission, but between the commissions and the law firms that serve the regulated industries.

What better experience is there for an attorney practicing before a regulatory commission, Goulden asks rhetorically, than actual service with that commission?

A more sophisticated theory suggesting the "capture" of individual regulators is what might be called an "identity theory." The regulatory commissioners and staff members, according to this view, develop a habitual tendency to agree with industry positions and representatives. In their study of the Federal Communications Commission, Nicholas Longley and Erwin Krasnow (1978, pp. 38-39) suggest that:

> On a day-to-day basis, Commissioners are forced to immerse themselves in the field they are supposed to regulate; however, the line between gaining a familiarity with an industry's problems and becoming biased thereby in favor of the industry is perilously thin. It is difficult for Commissioners and their staff to operate closely with an industry without coming to see its problems in industry terms.

Political economists have dealt with this question of the motivations of individual regulators through yet another theory, that of "self-interest maximizing models." Roger Noll suggests (Noll, 1971) that for commissions to be "successful" is for their orders to stand. In seeking success, therefore, they design orders that are less likely to be appealed, and if appealed are less likely to be overturned. As a result, Noll argues, the commissions shape their actions so as to offer enough that is desirable from the industry perspective to assure that the industry will be cautious about seeking judicial intervention to overturn their orders. Furthermore, Noll might have added, it is likely that such a protective posture by commissions will result in hesitancy to move far away from decisions following court-tested patterns.

At bottom, Noll suggests, the behavior of regulatory commissions must be understood on the basis of the behaviors of their members. He shows how a maximizing model concerning the individual commissioners can help explain the overall maximizing be-

33

havior of the commissions themselves. The individual
commissioner is motivated to derive the greatest possible benefit from his service on the commission.
That goal is most easily fulfilled by minimizing the
challenges the commission may pose to the regulated
industry. Noll argues that there is no political gain
derivable from regulation that threatens industry interests. His premise is that the electorate is not
attentive to the regulatory process, while the industry is constantly watching its actions with an
eagle eye. Thus vigorous regulation will only draw
the hostility of the industry, while bringing no attention from the electorate which could potentially
be translated into votes. The industry, however, can
bring challenges in court, can mobilize votes (through
employees and other economically involved citizens),
and can offer a secure future for the individual regulator through industry-related employment. "Since
there is little political gain in effective regulation," Noll concludes (Noll, 1971, p. 1031), "ineffective regulation will result--for there is political
gain (votes and campaign contributions from individuals
associated with the regulated industries) to be had
there."

Professors Russell and Shelton have developed a
similar but more detailed model (Russell and Shelton,
1974) of the behavior of regulators, based on a number of explicit assumptions. One is that a regulator
will want to insure his post-commission future. In
this regard, skills, contacts, and knowledge of the
regulatory process are an asset which can only be
realized in a future industry-related position. Another assumption is that the regulator will undertake
to survive in his present position. To achieve this
end, Russell and Shelton suggest that it is necessary
to form and to retain a political coalition which will
protect the regulator when decisions adversely affect
some parties. A third assumption is that the regulator is concerned not to violate his views of what is
right or wrong. Variations of these assumptions have
been employed by other authors also in attempting to
describe regulatory behavior.

Pursuing the first two assumptions, Russell and
Shelton argue that regulators can be classified under
three types: (a) those whose actions favor the regulated industry, (b) those whose actions favor con-

34

sumers, and (c) those who pursue the public interest defined as optimal resource-allocation given the existing income distribution (Pareto optimality). They postulate that regulators tend to view the amount of funds expended by competing groups in the regulatory process as a guide to likely later benefits to be achieved from identifying with one of the three types and its accompanying interests. As a result, Russell and Shelton argue, the largest number of regulators are advocates for utilities, a smaller number for consumers, and virtually none for the public interest (defined as Pareto optimality). Utilities can spend large amounts of money on the regulatory process because these funds are tax deductible and can be included in the cost of service. It is much more difficult for consumer groups to bring an equivalent amount of resources to bear for their purposes. The public interest, however, has no voice at all, because gains from its pursuit would be spread so thinly over the whole economy as to offer no incentive for any particular group to pursue.

Russell and Shelton point out that their assumptions imply that the regulator must be perceived by his colleagues and staff as having a constituency with sufficient clout not to be ignored. They observe that a commissioner with only a single base of support, whose actions are consistent only with the interests of that constituency, will be perceived as biased and with limited influence. As a result, they argue, commissioners attempt to develop a coalition of supporters from among the regulated firms and from subsets of consumers. The process of coalition-building includes the provision of services below cost to specific groups of customers (cross-subsidization), which tends (1) to create client groups who actively support or do not actively oppose the regulators, and (2) to increase industry profit by promoting expansion and improving the profit rate of the regulated firm. Another likely result is (3) satisfaction of the regulator's motives for doing what he thinks right (per assumption three), since socially disadvantaged persons often are included in the subsidized groups.

Russell and Shelton argue further that the regulator who decides to promote consumers interests also supports cross-subsidization while, in contrast, the "public interest" regulator will oppose all cross sub-

sidization and thus have few allies. The result, in
many cases, is that the concerns of the regulator who
pursues the interests of the regulated industry are
compatible with those of the regulator who pursues
the interests of the consumer, so that these officials
tend to ally themselves by cross-subsidization and to
exclude those who promote the public interest.

THE CHALLENGE OF REGULATORY THEORY

According to the Conventional Theory which provides official justification for the regulation of
"natural monopolies," as we have seen, the purpose of
regulation is to provide maximum benefit to society
from industries "affected with a public interest."
This amounts to allowing such industries the advantages of exclusive provision of services in their al-
loted areas while maintaining prices at a level representative of a competitive market. The possibility
of this purpose being achieved depends upon independence of the regulatory body not only from political
interference but also from domination by the regulated
industry.

Academic theories of regulation, for all their
variety, argue unaminously that this essential independence cannot be maintained, since regulatory commissions tend ineluctably to be "captured" by the industries they regulate. The academic theories differ
on what brings about this inevitable "capture." According to structural accounts of regulation, the
first of the three main versions examined above, the
organization and developmental nature of the commissions are the main factors leading to their loss of
autonomy. Policy accounts of regulation, on the other
hand, while maintaining emphasis upon impersonal aspects of the regulatory process, locate the variable
primarily responsible for "capture" by industry in a
faulty conceptualization of the regulatory function.
According to these theories, the guidelines provided
by empowering legislation are either so vague or so
misdirected that the regulators have to rely upon the
interests of the industry itself for a clear conception of their proper goals.

In contrast with both structural and policy accounts are the so-called "individual behavior" the-

36

ories of regulation, emphasizing the temptations and incentives by which the individual regulator is motivated in performing his role. Since neither monetary nor political gains can be achieved by identifying with the public interest abstractly conceived, the regulator is driven to seek alignment with groups capable of bestowing tangible rewards. In the preponderance of cases, this means alignment with the industry he is supposed to regulate.

Academic theory of regulation allows a bleak prospect at best of the capacity of the independent regulatory commission to represent the public interest effectively and in the long run. The prospect becomes even bleaker when we recall that demands upon the regulatory process from the public sector are becoming more extensive as well as more insistent. In the area of electric power regulation in particular, state commissions are under increasing pressure not only to restrain what the public sees as unjustified and too frequent rate increases but also to discourage wasteful consumption of power by large users and to take an active hand in the consideration of environmental impacts. These demands call for deviation from time-honored practices such as declining block rate structures and unquestioning support of new construction. If the complicity of the commissions with the industry they regulate is as extensive and inevitable as the academic theories portray it, the institution of the independent regulatory agency must be judged inadequate to meet the needs of contemporary American society.

If the academic theories have made their case that "capture" is an inevitable byproduct of the regulatory process, then the only hope the American public has of being effectively represented in major decisions regarding energy production and distribution is predicated on either increased government intervention (e.g., further price controls, or nationalization of energy industries) or radical restructuring of regulatory mechanisms. Since neither step seems at all likely given the political climate in the nation today, the American public has considerable stake in these theories being proven wrong.

There are two basic reasons, we believe, for being suspicious about the results of the academic the-

ories, apart from the details of their disagreements.
One is that these theories as a group are excessively
abstract, relying upon assumptions largely unsupported by empirical research. The other is that these
theories leave out of account the one variable that
would have to play a dominant role in the regulatory
process if this process were to function according
to the intent of its empowering statutes.

The variable that has been left out of account
is the set of values the individual regulator brings
to his task, which both shape the goals he sets out
to accomplish and govern his interaction with the regulated industry. In a word, the academic theories ignore considerations of professional ethics. By leaving out of account the factor of personal values which
must be influential if the regulatory process is to be
expected to work at all, it is a foregone conclusion
that the academic theories will find that process un-
workable as it stands.

We hasten to forestall an obvious objection on
behalf of the academic theories, which goes as follows. In accounting for the "capture" of regulators
by the regulated industries, whether on the basis of
structure, policy, or regulatory behavior, the academic theories in effect are taking the values of
individual regulators into account, for "capture" is
basically a matter of aligning one's values with those
of the industry. In the case of the "identity theory"
in particular, the objection continues, individual
values are involved explicitly, since the theory is
articulated in terms of the regulators' incentives and
motivations.

The answer to this objection is that in all the
academic theories the values of the individual regulators are treated, if at all, as dependent variables which may be swayed one way or another in response to pressures from the regulatory environment.
In the case of the "identity theory" in particular,
although its account is expressed in terms of values
of a motivational character, these are values which
make the individual particularly responsive to opportunities offering prestige or monetary gain. In none
of these theories, the "identity theory" included, are
personal values represented as variables which could
enable the individual regulator to resist temptations

38

from the regulatory environment that would impede a proper performance of his professional function. As mentioned above, it is precisely these values that must be operative if the regulatory process is to work as intended by its empowering legislation. Our complaint with the academic theories is not that they make no room for values at all, but rather that they do not leave room for the possibility that professional values might act as independent factors enabling the individual regulator to pursue his career without joining forces with the regulated industry.

A more subtle objection on behalf of the academic theories is that our complaint assumes that professional values of this sort in fact can have an effect in the performance of the individual regulator. If the pressures of cooptation are as powerful as the academic theories make out, then the notion that professional or ethical values of any sort might make an appreciable difference is just a matter of wishful thinking. That this is the case might be regretable, but constitutes no objection to the academic theories.

Our response to this latter objection is one of clarification. We are not assuming at the outset that professional and ethical values enable individual members of regulatory commissions to resist the temptation of joining forces with industry. Our complaint, rather, is that the academic theories assume that they do not have this effect and that this assumption is not backed by empirical data.

Our approach to the question of capture involves no prior assumptions about the capacity of individual regulators to remain independent agents. Instead we have posed a series of hypotheses for empirical testing, the results of which should indicate whether and under what conditions this capacity is present in the particular commission we have chosen as paradigm. To the extent that this case is typical in essential respects, the results can be extrapolated to other regulatory bodies.

These hypotheses, as specified in the chapter following, have been generated out of a conception of the regulatory process which stands in contrast both with the three major forms of academic theory discussed above and with the Conventional Theory of regula-

39

tion itself. According to this conception, the structure and policies of regulation are compatible both with capture of the individual regulators and of the commissions themselves, as predicted by the academic theories, and with exercise of the regulatory process in defense of the public interest, as traditionally envisaged by the Conventional Theory. The critical variable determining which alternative results is the configuration of values of the individual regulators.

To the extent that this conception is upheld, its response to the challenge of the academic theories is that when the "wrong" persons staff the commissions then indeed they are subject to capture, whether for reasons of policy or structure or personal behavior. If staffed by the "right" people, however, the commissions remain capable of performing the function for which they were originally intended. That is, the commissions remain effective advocates of the public interest. The difference between "right" and "wrong" in this connection is a matter of the value-orientations of the persons involved.

Although opposed to the academic theories discussed above, this conception of regulation is not a return to the Conventional Theory. In particular, it does not share with that theory the notion that the public interest is adequately protected by simulating the effects of a competitive market. In this time of energy shortage and environmental hazard, the public interest cannot be identified simply with economic benefits. The welfare of the public may depend as well upon a more fragile set of conditions, which can be maintained only by restraining our current profligate use of our limited energy resources. What specific conditions constitute the public interest, however, is not a topic of the present inquiry.

At stake in the analysis that follows are (1) the adequacy of the academic theories as accounts of the regulatory process, and (2) the adequacy of the regulatory process itself as serving the purpose for which it was intended. Adequacy in the second respect, as we have noted, requires inadequacy in the first.

The chapter following describes the methodology by which our inquiry was conducted.

40

NOTES

1. Unlike most scholarly writing in the social sciences, the literature on regulation is written with the policymaker directly in mind and is more often concerned with prescription than with description and analysis.

REFERENCES

Averch, H. and Johnson, L. (1962), "Behavior of the Firm Under Regulatory Constraint," American Economic Review, Vol. 52, December, pp. 1052-1069.

Barnes, I. (1942), The Economics of Public Utility Regulation, Appleton, Century, Crofts, New York.

Bernstein, M. (1955), Regulating Business by Independent Commissions, Princeton University Press, Princeton, N.J.

Bonbright, J. (1961), Principles of Public Utility Regulation, Columbia University Press, New York.

Davis, K.C. (1969), Discretionary Justice, Louisiana State University Press, Baton Rouge, Louisiana.

Dixon, R.G., Jr. (1975), "Independent Commissions and Political Responsibility," Administrative Law Review, Vol. 27, Winter, pp. 1-16.

Engler, R. (1961), The Politics of Oil, Macmillan, New York.

Ford Foundation Energy Policy Project (1974), A Time to Choose, Ballinger Publishing Co., Cambridge, Mass.

Friedman, M. (1962), Capitalism and Freedom, University of Chicago Press, Chicago.

Friendly, H. (1962), The Federal Administrative Agencies, Harvard University Press, Cambridge, Mass.

Goulden, J. (1972), The Superlawyers, Weybright and Talley, New York.

Huntington, S.P. (1952), "The Marasmus of the I.C.C.," Yale Law Journal, Vol. 61, April, pp. 467-509.

Insull, S. (1924), Public Utilities in Modern Life: Selected Speeches (1914-1923), privately printed, Chicago.

Kohlmeier, L.M., Jr. (1969), The Regulators, Harper and Row, New York.

Krasnow, E. and Longley, L. (1978), The Politics of Broadcast Regulation, St. Martin's Press, New York.

McConnell, G. (1966), Private Power and American Democracy, Knopf, New York.

New State Ice Co. v. Liebmann (1931) 76 U.C. 479.

Noll, R. (1971), "The Economics and Politics of Regulation," Virginia Law Review, Vol. 57, September, pp. 1016-1032.

Petersen, H. (1975), "An Empirical Test of Regulatory Effects," The Bell Journal of Economics and Management Science, Vol. 6, Spring, pp. 111-126.

President's Committee (1937), Report with Special Studies, U.S. Government Printing Office, Washington.

Russell, M. and Shelton, R.B. (1974), "A Model of Regulatory Agency Behavior," Public Choice, Winter, pp. 47-52.

Samuels, W.J. (1972), "Public Utilities and the Theory of Power," in Russell (ed.) Perspectives on Public Regulation, Southern Illinois University Press, Carbondale, Illinois, pp. 1-33.

Schwartz, B. (1959), The Professor and the Commissions, knopf, New York.

Sheshinski, E. (1971), "Welfare Aspects of a Regulatory Constraint," American Economic Review, Vol. 61, March, pp. 175-178.

Spann, R. (1974), "Rate of Return Regulation and Efficiency in Production: An Empirical Test of
the Averch-Johnson Thesis," The Bell Journal of
Economics and Management Science, Vol. 5, Spring,
pp. 38-52.

U.S. Commission on the Organization of the Executive
Branch (1948), Task Force Report on Regulatory
Commissions, U.S. Government Printing Office,
Washington.

Zajac, E. (1970), "A Geometric Treatment of Averch-
Johnson's Behavior of the Firm Model," American
Economic Review, Vol. 60, March, pp. 117-125.

2 Methodology

THE RESEARCH PROBLEM

According to the Conventional Theory of regulation, we have seen, one purpose of regulation is to secure for the public the advantages of obtaining essential goods and services from a single supplier without the disadvantages of being dependent upon an unrestrained monopoly. At the same time, the Conventional Theory sees regulation as a way of encouraging the regulated industry to provide fair and reliable service, by guaranteeing to it a reasonable return on investment. According to the various theories of regulation produced by social scientists in recent decades, by contrast, regulatory commissions inevitably are rendered incapable of serving this function over the full span of their careers because they tend eventually to align their interests with the industries they regulate.

A guiding supposition behind the research reported in this volume is that both the academic theories and the Conventional Theory leave an important element out of account. The missing factor is the set of values represented on a given regulatory commission--in particular the values guiding the thinking of individual regulators in matters affecting the public interest. Our conjecture was that a group of regulators guided by a strong set of socially oriented

44

values would be able to resist capture by the regulated industry, whereas another group lacking this guidance might tend rather quickly to identify with the interests of the industry they are supposed to regulate.

Our conjecture, in brief, was that the behavior of regulatory agencies does not necessarily follow the description of either of these two major theoretical accounts, and that the direction a given agency takes is a function of the values of its individual members. Our study was structured to test this conjecture in the form of a series of explicit hypotheses, each capable of being confirmed or disconfirmed on the basis of empirical data.

One purpose of the present chapter is to articulate these hypotheses carefully, and to describe the data-collection instruments by which they were tested. A supplementary task is to define how we use the ambiguous term 'value'.

First in order, however, is to describe both the history and the present organization of the Illinois Commerce Commission, the particular case chosen as subject of the present study. Choice of a single agency as a research case was dictated by the need to correlate the value-orientations of individual regulators with the decisions of the group to which they all contribute. Although it would be desirable to have included a wider range of cases in a more comprehensive study, and may in fact be possible to do this on some future occasion, the disadvantages of being limited to a single case were minimized by choosing a particular agency with a long history of performance and an outstanding reputation for integrity and public consciousness. If it turns out that independence from industry and support of the public interest remain dominant factors in the conception of purpose motivating this agency after its many years of operation, the academic theories predicting capture will be to a degree discredited. On the other hand, if the dominant motivations of an agency with this reputation should be found largely to reflect the interests of the regulated industry, this finding will tend to refute the Conventional Theory. Moreover, if empirical support is to be found for our conjecture that the values of the individual regulators can make an important difference in the performance of the commission they constitute, an agency like the ICC is the most likely place to set about looking for it.

In these theoretical respects, accordingly, the ICC is an exemplary research case, given the present need to limit our study to a particular agency. A practical justification of this research case is provided by considerations of accessibility, and by the fact that a parallel study of a major utility under the jurisdiction of the ICC has already been completed and offers interesting opportunities of comparison.

THE ILLINOIS COMMERCE COMMISSION

Electric power come under regulation in Illinois with the creation of the Public Utilities Commission in 1913. Prior to that time, franchises to provide electric power were under the control of municipalities and in most cases were not exclusive (Davis, 1974, p. 116). The commission established in the 1913 act was charged with the regulation of all public utilities in the state. It superseded the former Railroad and Warehouse Commission which had been regulating railroads and warehouses since 1871 (Mueller, 1966, p. xii).

In 1921 the commission again was reorganized and given its present name of the Illinois Commerce Commission. Regulatory powers of the ICC extend to some 338 public utilities, in addition to over 18,000 motor carriers (Dowling et al., 1976, p. 3.5). Table 2.1 lists the various types of utilities regulated in 1976, with the numbers of companies in each category, along with the comparable figures for 1967.

Mueller (1966, p. xvii) summarizes the general powers and duties of the Commission pertaining to public utilities under four headings:

(1) supervision of accounts, security issues and corporate transactions, (2) regulation of rates and service, (3) conduct of investigations and hearings, and (4) enforcement of the Act and of Commission orders thereunder.

46

The Commission's most recent Annual Report (ICC, 1967, p. 4)[1] spells out these duties in greater detail:

> In executing these [regulatory powers]
> the Commission grants certificates to
> new utilities and extensions to the cer-
> tificates of existing utilities; con-
> trols utility rate making; requires
> utilities to provide adequate service
> and reasonable safety to patrons, employ-
> ees and the general public; supervises
> utility accounting and other financial
> matters; and provides a procedure for
> the disposition of complaints.

In the regulation of rates, the Commission has the power (subject to procedural limits) to modify or to reject proposed rate schedules, or even to modify schedules presently in effect. It has a clear statutory mandate to reduce rates that yield more than a reasonable profit, and more nebulous mandates to increase rates that seem likely to impair a utility's solvency and to revise classifications that seem unfair.

Although the regulation of motor carriers is described by Commission personnel as fairly routine (Dowling et al., 1976, p. 4.25), the regulation of electric utilities is less subject to standard procedures. The tendency of the Commission has been to handle the latter on a case-by-case basis, without establishing routine procedures and policies. This tendency has been encouraged by the relatively small number of individual utilities being regulated.

Certain procedures with respect to rate cases, however, are required by statute. Rate proceedings are initiated with the filing of new tariffs by the utility company, along with a public announcement of filing. The effective date of such proposed tariffs is thirty days after the date of filing. Within this time the proposed rates may be allowed to go into effect automatically, or the Commission may suspend them for a ten month period to hold hearings on their propriety and reasonableness (S. 36). Such hearings are held by a Hearing Examiner.

Recommendations at conclusion of rate hearings

47

are conveyed by the Hearing Examiner to the Commissioners, but do not become part of the public record (Dowling et al., 1976, p. 4.23). The Commissioners may request further information or clarification as they deem necessary.[2] If no contrary determination has been reached by the end of the ten-month suspension period, the proposed rates then become effective (S. 36).

Decisions of the Commission are subject to typical provisions for judicial review. The court may not substitute its discretion for that of the Commission, but may set aside Commission action which it finds to be unreasonable or unsupported by evidence. It may either reverse or uphold Commission orders, but has no power to modify their content.

Composition of the ICC is established by statute. The Commission is composed of five Commissioners appointed by the Governor on a bipartisan basis with the approval of the state Senate for five year terms on a staggered schedule (National Association of Regulatory Commissions, 1976, p. 607). One of the five is appointed by the Governor as Chairman, serving in this capacity at the Governor's pleasure. At the time the present study began, one of the Commission seats was vacant and the recently elected Republican Governor Thompson had announced his intention to fill the vacancy by appointing a new Chairman.[3]

In addition to those of the five Commissioners, the position of Secretary is established by law. This is an appointive office which, according to the Dowling report (1976, p. 4.14), has only vestigial significance today, its sole remaining function being the authentication of Commission documents. It has been recommended that this position be abolished, at a budgetary saving of about $25,000 a year (Dowling et al., 1976, p. 4.14).

The Commission is empowered to employ a staff. This staff has grown considerably over the years. Two-hundred forty-four positions were authorized for fiscal year 1976-77. About one-fourth of the staff members are professionals (accountants, lawyers, engineers, and administrators); the remainder are clerks, typists, and so forth. The Commission has requested an additional twenty-three positions for

48

1977-78, most of these slated for the utility sections.

The Chairman has traditionally functioned as chief executive officer of the Commission, with full administrative authority. However, this authority is largely informal and unspecified in the statutes. It was recommended recently that this informal arrangement be ratified by statute (Dowling et al., 1976, p. 4.12).

Organization of the Commission staff appears to have varied over the years, apparently at the pleasure of the various Chairmen, acting under their statutory power to set up whatever organizational structure they consider appropriate to the accomplishment of the Commission's duties (ICC, 1967, p. 6). In 1967 there were eight sections, three reporting to the Secretary and the other five to the Administrative Assistant to the Chairman. One of the latter sections, Engineering, included five divisions corresponding to the various regulated public utilites (railroad, electric, gas, telephone, and water-sewer). The appointment of a new chairman in April, 1969, was followed by a change to a more horizontal structure, with separate sections for each of these utilities.

Marvin Lieberman became Chairman in January 1973. In August 1976, he appointed a special task force to conduct an internal management review. The report of that task force, presented in December 1976, included a number of recommendations for organizational restructuring, some of which were in the process of implementation at the time the present study began.

As noted in this report (Dowling et al., 1976, p. 3.4), the 1976 management review recommends a return to a structure very much like that which existed in 1967. The existing organizational chart shows a rather shallow, lateral structure, with some thirteen different sections all reporting directly to the Chairman. The proposed restructuring would consolidate the various public utilities sections (involving 141 of the 244 staff members) under a single division, to be headed by a new Manager of Public Utilities.

Other important restructuring proposals include (1) establishment of a Division of the General Counsel

49

to provide legal advice to staff and Commissioners;
(2) creation of a Policy Analysis and Research Division to handle generic issues; and (3) consolidation
of the Hearing Examiners for public utilities and
motor carriers under one division, which would also
include a Process Section for the handling and main-
tenance of all Commission records (Dowling et al.,
1976, pp. 2.3 and 4.12-21). The first two proposals
represent logical extensions of two specialized positions created during Chairman Lieberman's tenure,
those of Technical Advisor for Legal Affairs and of
Energy Advisor.

Among organizational constraints affecting the
Commission, the most obvious is budgetary. In 1963
the Public Utilities Act was amended to establish the
Public Utility Fund, to be derived primarily from an
.08 percent tax on the gross revenues of all regulated public utilities. A similar fund was established
to defray the Commission's expenses in administering
the Motor Carrier Act. These special funds now support all Commission expenses, with the exception of
the salaries of the Commissioners and of the Secretary which are paid from general tax revenues (ICC,
1967, p. 12).

This 1963 legislation set a biennial ceiling of
$3.5 million for the Commission budget. This was
raised to the present $5.5 million in 1970. The 1976
internal management review recommended that this
spending limit be removed. Its argument was that removing the limit would permit a more adequate level
of expenditure without any increase in utility assess-
ments or other taxes, since under the current system
public utility revenues in excess of the limited ex-
penditures are refunded to the utilities in the form
of credits (Dowling et al., 1976, pp. 2.1, 4.2-3).

The Commission's limited financial resources are
reflected most significantly in relatively low staff
salaries, a continuing source of morale problems. As
of 1976, the salary of the Chairman was $37,500, those
of the other Commissioners $32,000 (Dowling et al.,
1976, p. 3.4). Salaries of professional staff range
from $12,000 to $28,000 a year, low in comparison with
salaries commanded by professional counterparts in the
private sector. Throughout the Dowling report there
are suggestions that the salary levels are too low to

attract and to retain high quality personnel (1976,pp.
4.23, 24, 34).[4] The same report goes on to argue that
inadequate compensation may put staff members, particularly Hearing Examiners, at a psychological disadvantage in dealing with industry representatives
(Dowling et al., 1976, pp. 4.25, 34).

Inadequate funding results in understaffing, so
that recent increases in Commission workload have not
been met by proportional increases in staff. For example, the case load in the Accounts and Finance Section has increased from 3.5 per employee in 1972 to
6.5 in 1976 (Dowling et al., 1976, p. 4.29). Further,
the size and specialization of the Commission staff
offer only restricted avenues for career advancement,
and in some staff positions the nature of the work
provides little challenge for professional development.

A special logistical problem of the Illinois
Commerce Commission is the separation of the state
capital at Springfield from the major population and
industrial center in Chicago. While the main base of
operations is in the capital, the Commission maintains
an office in Chicago to accommodate the needs of the
upstate population. The Commissioners are in Chicago
for several days during alternate weeks. In addition,
top administrative staff have to commute between the
two offices frequently, an arrangement which is quite
costly in both time and money. Moreover, a recent
move toward fully open deliberations (made voluntarily in anticipation of the enactment of sunshine
laws) may be expected to intensify this problem by
requiring a larger number of staff members to be present throughout each Commission proceeding (Dowling
et al., 1976, p. 4.11).

DATA COLLECTION

During the summer and fall of 1977, sixty-three
persons presently or formerly associated with the ICC
as Commissioners or professional staff members were
invited to participate in our study by completing a
series of questionnaires and standardized tests. Of
these sixty-three, a total of forty-five persons responded to all or part of the survey series, giving
an overall response rate of 71 percent.

This sample was not drawn on a random basis. Individuals were strategically selected to include all
present and living past commissioners, most of the
professional staff dealing exclusively with the regulation of electric utilities, and some professional
staff members from each other section of the Commission. Although our primary concern was with the regulation of electric power, staff members from other
sections were included because their views could have
an indirect impact on electric power regulation. The
initial list of participants was drawn up according to
our guidelines by an administrative assistant of the
ICC. A few additional persons were added later at
the suggestion of other participants or at their own
request.

In all, four commissioners, five former commissioners, and fifty-four staff members were invited
to participate in the study. Of these, two commissioners[5], three former commissioners, and forty staff
members responded fully or in part. For purposes of
data analysis, however, no distinctions were drawn
among roles within the Commission. From one point of
view this may appear problematic, since official decisions are made by the commissioners and not by the
group as a whole. On the other hand, to picture the
commissioners as functioning in a vacuum is an obvious
misrepresentation. Not only do key staff members have
essential responsibility in putting together briefs
in behalf of the public interest which the hearing
examiners and commissioners rely upon in formulating
their decisions, but also groups of staff members
have authority to initiate proposals for policy change
(such as different rate structures). Moreover, as
mentioned previously, staff members play influential
roles in the open hearings recently initiated by the
ICC, and thereby contribute significantly to the public posture assumed by the Commission on issues within its jurisdiction. For our purposes, it is realis-
tic to view the decision-structure of the Commission
as a series of concentric circles with the commissioners playing the central role, rather than as a
pyramid with only the commissioners exercising a decision-making function.

Another reason for not distinguishing key staff
from commissioners in our data reduction, which practically speaking is conclusive in itself, is that

there are too few commissioners (even if all had responded) to permit statistical analysis of their responses separately. The need for confidentiality was
also a consideration. In the discussion that follows,
the term 'regulator' will be used to refer to members
of our sample without respect to particular role within the Commission. When role is pertinent, more specific designations such as 'commissioner', 'hearing
examiner', and 'engineering supervisor' will be employed.

Briefly profiled, the sample as obtained is predominantly white (83 percent) and male (81 percent),
with a median age of 38 years. At the time these data
were collected, the average (median) respondent had
been with the ICC for four years. Most came from
previous employment in government (eight) or in private industry (seven from non-regulated industry, five
from regulated). For seven respondents, the Commission is the first full-time employer.

The majority identify themselves as lawyers (22
percent), engineers (24 percent) or administrators
(16 percent). They are highly educated; 25 percent
hold law degrees and another 16 percent have master's
degrees or equivalent. Only 13 percent of the sample lack the baccalaureate degree, and most of these
have had some college education. Politically, most
identify themselves as independent (33 percent) or
decline to give a political preference (29 percent).
Of the 33 percent who report a preference for one of
the major parties, Democrats outnumber Republicans
by a ratio of 2 to 1 (22 percent and 11 percent of
the sample, respectively).

Data were gathered by administering three standardized values tests and two written questionnaires
to all participants. During June 1977, respondents
were asked to complete the Study of Values (Allport
et al., 1970), the California Life Goals Evaluation
Schedules (Hahn, 1969), and a twenty-six page questionnaire constructed especially for use in this
study (see Appendix A). In August 1977, the same
respondents were asked to complete the Value Survey
(Rokeach, 1967) and a second questionnaire calling
for evaluative judgments in response to eight hypothetical decision-situations (see Appendix B).

Both the Study of Values and the California Life
Goals Evaluation Schedules (CLGES) were used in the
earlier study of electric utility executives conducted by this research group. Since a full discussion
of the reasons for selecting these tests, along with
a summary of reliability and validity data, appears
in the final report of the earlier study, Values in
the Electric Power Industry (Sayre, 1977, pp. 203-
208), this material is not repeated here. The Study
of Values yields six interest-area scores, representing the relative strength of the respondent's interest in theoretical, economic, aesthetic, social, political, and religious matters. The CLGES consists of
ten different scales derived from 150 opinion items
representing the personal life goals of esteem, profit, fame, power, leadership, security, social service, interesting experiences, self-expression, and
independence.

The Rokeach Value Survey was not included in the
earlier study. It consists of thirty-six value items
arranged in two groups of eighteen each, which Rokeach calls "terminal values" and "instrumental values" (Rokeach, 1973). The respondent is instructed
to rearrange the two alphabetical lists so as to rank
the values in order of personal importance. In the
present study, Form D of the Value Survey was used,
requiring the respondent to manipulate gummed labels
containing the value terms and brief clarifying descriptions.[6]

While none of the standardized tests used provides a perfect capsulization of the values of the
repondents, taken together they enable us to construct
a profile of the individual's goals and preferences
as they appear in a wide range of situations. There
are two additional advantages to using standarized
tests as a part of our survey package: they allow
us to relate our findings to other studies in the
literature and they provide us with norms for com-
parision based on occupational and other relevant variables.

In addition to the tests by Allport and Hahn, the
first phase of the survey included a twenty-six page
questionnaire specially constructed for the present
study. About three-fourths of this questionnaire consists of items calling for choice among specified re-

sponses. Remaining items are open-ended questions
requiring answers in the form of lists or statements
composed by the respondent. A number of items in both
groups had appeared in the earlier study of utility
executives, permitting us to make some comparisons
across the two populations. Although we tried to make
the task of completing the questionnaire as painless
as possible, the fairly slow pace at which the returns
came in (as well as a number of explicit comments)
suggests that the respondents found the instrument
unduly long. In view of this problem, the relatively
high response rate appears as impressive evidence of
the participants' strong desire to cooperate with the
study.

A second questionnaire was distributed as part of
the second phase of the survey. This instrument,
which we will refer to as the "scenario questionnaire," consisted of eight hypothetical cases or scenarios about decisions pertaining to electric power,
each decision involving an ethical dilemma. After
reading each case, the respondent was asked to tell
whether he or she agreed or disagreed with the decision which was made, and then to explain the reasoning behind this response. For our purposes, these
open-ended statements of reasoning are particularly
interesting for the ethical perspectives which they
reveal.

Six of the eight scenarios (numbers one through
six) exactly or nearly duplicate items included in the
study of utility executives. These were chosen not
only for the relevance of their content, but also because they had yielded fairly homogeneous responses in
the earlier study. Thus they offered a clear-cut basis for comparison between utility personnel and regulators. A more detailed discussion of the development
of the scenarios and the logic behind them can be
found in Values in the Electric Power Industry (Sayre,
1977, pp. 199-203).

In addition to the survey data just described,
other valuable data were obtained from a variety of
documentary sources, as well as through direct observation by the members of the study group. One source
was particularly useful and merits special mention
here. We have already mentioned the task force appointed in 1976 by Chairman Lieberman to do an inter-

nal management study for the Commission. The report
compiled by this group proved to be an invaluable
source of information on the current organizational
status of the Commission and offered important insights into prevailing attitudes as well. One of the
authors, John Urban, served as liaison to the present
project.

VALUES AS GUIDES FOR CHOICE

Since the term 'value' carries many different
meanings in ordinary discourse, it is important to be
explicit about our own use of the term. Among common
senses of 'value' that will not be employed here are
that of monetary worth, that of capacity for confer-
ring benefits, and that of individuals instantiating
variables (in mathematics and logic). Values in the
present context are conceived instead as incentives
for action and as guides for choice.

In his Value Survey administered as part of this
study, Rokeach discusses two types of value. One is
what he calls terminal values, defined as "desirable
end-states of existence" (Rokeach, 1973, p. 7). Examples of terminal values are national security, freedom, peace and self-respect. What he calls instrumental values are defined as "desirable modes of conduct" (ibid.), examples of which are courage, helpfulness, honesty and obedience. The difference is
between desirable states of affairs in one's own life
or in the world at large and desirable qualities of
character or personality.

Values in both senses are incentives. To value
a world at peace, for instance, is to treat that state
of affairs as a desirable one, and to act when appropriate for its fulfillment. To value honesty, in similar fashion, is to choose courses of action when an
option is present that avoid deceit and misrepresentation. In this respect, values constitute priorities
for choice among alternative courses of action. Valuing a world at peace, one will give precedence to
actions enhancing that state of affairs over actions
with results considered less desirable. Valuing honesty, one will prefer courses of action exemplifying
that quality over other courses exemplifying qualities
to which one is indifferent. Values in this sense are

56

norms or guides for choice among possible courses of action.

Alternatives for action can arise in which values enter into competition. Facing a possible course of action in which enhancing national security would involve dishonesty, for instance, one will choose to pursue or not to pursue that course depending upon which value carries the higher priority. A person who ranks honesty over national security is said to have a value-orientation different from that of another person who ranks national security over honesty.

Inadequate as these remarks may be toward a definition of values responding to the problems raised in the technical literature of sociology and philosophy,[7] they permit a definition suitable for present purposes. As used on this study, the term 'value' refers to an attitude toward a quality of character or state of affairs that serves as a guide for action: (1) providing incentive for acting so as to exemplify that quality or to enhance that state, (2) guiding choice of rank that quality or state relative to qualties and states associated with other values, and (3) applicable as a norm for assessing that quality or state as "good," "right" or otherwise desirable.

In the study reported here, we have been concerned to characterize and to measure the values held by key members of a particular state regulatory commission. The values primarily in question are such as can be related in some clear fashion to the public interest--such values as economic growth, environmental soundness, justice and equity.

As noted in our brief review of the history and legal background of regulation in this country, the commissioners and staff of a typical regulatory agency are mandated to serve the public by controlling rates and by preventing discriminatory marketing practices within a given class of customer. They are mandated to serve the regulated industry, in turn, by assuring reasonable profits and by protecting established industry from costly competition. According to the Conventional Theory, at least, performance of these tasks is a matter of gathering facts, weighing testimony, and issuing decisions which duplicate as closely as possible the effects that would come about in a com-

petitive market. However recondite and complex the
factors which enter into these decisions, they are at
least considered to be decisions governed by explicit
standards rather than by the personal values of regulators.

In practice, however, things are not that simple.
For one thing, duplicating the effects of the free
market is seldom a matter of expert calculation as the
Conventional Theory supposes--even in cases where regulators accept this conception of what their task is
about. For another thing, regulators of the electric
power industry traditionally have rendered decisions
for which explicit standards are notoriously absent--
for instance, decisions about proper siting of new
generating facilities. Most importantly, however, in
the regulatory climate of the present decade regulators are being called upon to defend the public interest in the light of concerns that are not exclusively
economic in character. They are being called upon,
for example, to take into account the social and environmental effects of various rate structures. Not
only are such environmental and social concerns totally foreign to the Conventional Theory, but they are
also concerns which cannot be met in terms of explicit
and accepted standards. In brief, such environmental
and social concerns bring into relevance the values of
the regulators in a way that goes beyond whatever
technical engineering and economic expertise they
bring to the regulatory task.

The conjecture behind this study, as noted above,
is that values are primary factors determining (i)
whether a performance of a given regulatory agency
will follow the pattern laid out by the Conventional
Theory, in which regulation works for the public interest conventionally defined; (ii) will follow the
pattern of the academic theories, in which regulation
serves the interests of the regulated industries; or
(iii) will follow some other pattern instead. In the
following section we formulate the particular hypotheses through which this conjecture will be tested. Beyond the outcome of this test, however, it is clear
that the value-orientations dominating a given regulatory agency will be strongly influential in determining how the agency responds to the environmental
and social demands which have arisen in the present
decade. This in itself warrants an attempt to under-

stand better the values present within the Illinois
Commerce Commission--an agency whose concern for the
public interest enjoys wide repute.

HYPOTHESES TO BE TESTED

The following hypotheses were posed for empirical testing. Two of these hypotheses incorporate a
distinction between regulators who in their thought
patterns or decisions tend to favor utility interests
and those who do not favor the utilities in these respects. The first will be said to be "aligned," the
second to be "nonaligned." (The concept of alignment
will be further explicated in Chapter Three.)

> Hypothesis 1: A significant number of regula-
> tors on the ICC are nonaligned.

> Hypothesis 2: Nonaligned regulators hold per-
> sonal values which are signifi-
> cantly different from those held
> by aligned regulators.

Of particular interest in this study are values pertaining to the public interest, such as justice and
fairness. Such values play a role in traditional
ethical discussions of the social good, which may provide a basis for objective criticism of regulatory
decision-making. The third hypothesis is concerned
with alternative conceptions of the social good which
may be distinguished in the light of traditional ethical theory.

> Hypothesis 3: Nonaligned regulators hold values
> pertaining to the public interest
> which are ethically distinguish-
> able from those held by aligned
> regulators.

Hypothesis 1 will be confirmed if there are found
to be more than an isolated few regulators on the Commission who are nonaligned. Hypothesis 2 will be confirmed if it is found that nonaligned individuals hold
values which are statistically different from those of
aligned individuals, as indicated by the tests of
value-orientation.

Confirmation of Hypothesis 1 would be a result in opposition to the academic theories of regulation, since nonalignment is equivalent to not being "captured." Confirmation of Hypotheses 1 and 2 together would support our thesis that individual values are critical variables determining whether or not the regulatory process tends to support the regulated industry.

Positive results with these first two hypotheses, however, would not be adequate to sustain the basic conjecture that values can determine whether regulation in a particular context works to protect the public interest. The reason is that the notion of the public interest has never been adequately defined, and that what is actually in the public interest may be even more difficult to determine today than was the case when the Conventional Theory was originally formulated. To propose a testable hypothesis approximating what we would like ideally to find out, we have incorporated in our third hypothesis the notion of ethically distinguishable conceptions of the public interest. In proposing this hypothesis, we have not assumed that individual regulators subscribe explicitly to any particular ethical theory, or even are aware of the options ethical theory provides. What we have assumed is that an appreciable number of individual regulators--particularly those who are non-aligned--will entertain a conception of the public interest that is articulate and consistent enough to be correlated with one or another systematic conception of the social good provided by traditional ethical theory. In Chapter Five, we examine this hypothesis in two stages, first testing for differences between aligned and nonaligned regulators and then examining our findings in the light of ethical theory.[8]

NOTES

1. The Commission has not published a full-scale annual report since 1967, although financial and other reports have been regularly prepared. The 1976 internal management review recommended that monthly and annual reports be made by the Commission to the Governor and legislature and to the public (Dowling et al., 1976, p. 4.28).

2. It appears that recently-adopted "sunshine" policies have somewhat restricted the informal flow of information and ideas within the Commission, particularly at this stage of the rate review; but the internal management-review authors reported a generally favorable assessment of the new policies as they have been implemented in the other Commissions which they studied (Dowling et al., 1976, pp. 4.10-11).

3. About two months after the data collection phase of the project began (in August 1977), Chairman Marvin Lieberman submitted his resignation from the Commission. In September 1977, Governor Thompson appointed Charles P. Kocoras Chairman and Charles G. Stalon Commissioner, bringing the Commission back to full strength for the first time since December 1976. Helen S. Schmid, Alfred Reichman, and C. Burton Nelson continued as Commissioners.

4. This is by no means a new or unique problem for state regulatory commissions. In a 1916 address to a group of Iowa utility men, Samuel Insull, founder of Commonwealth Edison, expressed concern that regulatory bodies might lack the financial resources to employ competent personnel, a situation he feared would be detrimental to the regulated utilities. For this reason, among others, he preferred centralized state commissions to smaller-scale municipal bodies. Even then, he expressed concern that state-wide commissions might also lack adequate talent, for, he noted, "the state is not in the habit of bidding any such price for brains as public-utility corporations do..." (1924, pp. 58, 62).

5. One additional set of materials from a commissioner was received too late to be included in the data presented here.

6. Rokeach reports (1973, pp. 33-34) that this form of the test as proved to be the most reliable of the various forms which have been used (with reliabilities of .78-.80 and .70-.72 on terminal and instrumental values respectively, obtained from college student populations tested at intervals of three to seven weeks). Although he provides no explicit discussion of the test's validity, Rokeach does give an extended analysis of test findings for various subgroups in the population, with breakdowns by sex, age, racial, eco-

61

nomic and political groupings. These findings provide a reasonable discriminant validation of the two scales, over and above their considerable face validity.

7. Although both philosophers and social scientists have attempted to provide general accounts of the nature of values, neither have achieved results that have earned common acceptance even within the respective disciplines themselves. The sense of the term 'values' adopted above, nonetheless, is close to that of Kluckhohn (1954, p. 395) among sociologists and that of Baier (1969) among philosophers.

8. This technique of criticism, which we refer to as "ethical diagnostics," is fully discussed in Sayre (1977), pp. 238-43, in which context it is applied to the decision-making of Commonwealth Edison of Chicago.

REFERENCES

Allport, G.W., Vernon, P.E., and Lindzey, G. (1970), Study of Values, Third Edition, Houghton Mifflin Co., Boston.

Baier, K. (1969), "What is Value? An Analysis of the Concept," in Baier and Rescher (eds.), pp. 33-67.

Baier, K. and Rescher, N. (eds.) (1969), Values and the Future, The Free Press, New York.

Davis, D.H. (1974), Energy Politics, St. Martin's Press, New York.

Dowling, A., Urban, J., and Podlasek, R. (1976), An Internal Management Review of the Illinois Commerce Commission, Springfield, Illinois.

Hahn, M.E. (1969), The California Life Goals Evaluation Schedules, Western Psychological Services, Los Angeles.

Illinois Commerce Commission (ICC) (1967), Annual Report, Springfield, Illinois.

Insull, S. (1924), Public Utilities in Modern Life:
    Selected Speeches (1914-1923), privately printed,
    Chicago.

Kluckhohn, C. (1954), "Values and Value-Orientations
    in the Theory of Action; An Exploration in Defi-
    nition and Classification," in T. Parsons and E.
    Shils (eds.), Toward a General Theory of Action,
    Harvard University Press, Cambridge, 1954, pp.
    388-433.

Mueller, J.H. (1966), "Origin and Development of Pub-
    lic Utility Regulation in Illinois," Smith-Hurd
    Illinois Annotated Statutes, Chapter III-2/3,
    Burdette Smith Co, Chicago.

National Association of Regulatory Utility Commissions
    (1976), 1975 Annual Report on Utility and Carrier
    Regulation, Washington, D.C.

Rokeach, M. (1967), Value Survey, Halgren Tests, Sun-
    nyvale, California.

Rokeach, M. (1973), The Nature of Human Values, The
    Free Press, New York.

Sayre, K.M. (ed.) (1977), Values in the Electric Power
    Industry, University of Notre Dame Press, Notre
    Dame, Indiana.

TABLE 2.1
Principal Utilities Regulated by
the Illinois Commerce Commission
Types and Numbers, 1967 and 1976

Type of Utility	Number Under Regulation	
	1967 (Dec. 31, 1967)*	1976 (Jan. 1, 1976)**
Telephone	70	55
Gas and electric	24	33
Water-sewer	148	145
Telegraph	1	1
Steam heating	1	1
Barge	5	6
Mobile telephone	9	17
Motor carrier (property)	17,710	18,000
Motor carrier (passenger buses)	55	38
Railroad	68	61
Railway express	1	1
Pipelines	13	18

*1967 ICC Annual Report, p. 41 (adapted)
**Dowling et al., 1976 p. 3.5 (adapted)

3 Alignment in the ICC

The first hypothesis formulated for empirical testing is that a significant number of regulators in the Illinois Commerce Commission are not aligned with the interests of the electric utilities they regulate. Confirmation of this hypothesis would count as evidence against the several academic theories of regulation discussed in Chapter Two, each of which predicts the "capture" of regulators by the industries they regulate.

In Chapter One the term 'capture' was used, following the custom of the academic literature on the topic, to refer generally to the assimilation of the purposes and interests of the regulated industries by the regulators themselves. We have chosen to replace this term for the remainder of the discussion by the less pejorative term 'alignment', which we believe will allow a more nuanced analysis of the relationship between regulators and regulated. The term "capture" bears a sinister connotation which we consider too strong for some of the phenomena to which it is applied in the academic theories. These phenomena have one basic element in common: a failure of the regulatory system to work in the public interest as the conventional theory says it ought. As the following discussion should make clear, a number of the conditions which have been identified as either causes or indicators of "capture" are neither deliberate nor sinister in nature, nor prima facie contrary to the public interest.

In this chapter, we will first discuss various conceptions of alignment identifiable in the academic literature, together with the techniques which we have used to measure them. Then we will examine the extent to which the various forms of alignment are correlated with one another, and present the data testing the first hypothesis.

By 'alignment' we mean generally any consistent pattern of thought or behavior on the part of an individual regulator or commission which may be expected to support the interests, policies, or positions of the regulated industry. Since 'alignment' is being used as a replacement for the more tendentious term 'capture', it is noteworthy that the latter term has been used in a number of distinct and not necessarily correlated senses. The following list includes the most common meanings of 'capture' to be found in the academic literature:

(1) a consistent pattern of decisions by a commission that favor the interests of the regulated industry (e.g., Huntington, 1952; Schwartz, 1959)

(2) a conscious identification with and protection of the vested interests of the regulated industry on the part of the regulators (e.g., Bernstein, 1955)

(3) a close personal association between regulators and representatives of the regulated industry (e.g., Goulden, 1972; Kohlmeier, 1969; Schwartz, 1959)

(4) a pattern of dependence by the regulators on expertise and information supplied by the regulated industry (e.g., Krasnow and Longley, 1973; Engler, 1961; Schwartz, 1973)

(5) a persistent diversion of regulatory efforts away from substantial questions concerning the public interest through the proliferation

of procedural details and day-to-day problems (e.g., U.S. Comm., 1949; Goulden, 1972)

(6) perpetuation within the commission of a narrow and reactive conception of its role (U.S.
Comm., 1949; Bernstein, 1955; Engler, 1961)

(7) control of appointments and retention of
members of the commission through the exercise of political pressure by the regulated
industry (e.g., Friendly, 1962; Engler, 1961;
Huntington, 1952; Kohlmeier, 1969)

(8) exertion by the regulated industry of undue
influence upon individual regulators through
tangible or intangible inducements, especially through the expectation of future employment (Krasnow and Longley, 1973; Goulden,
1972)

It is a common practice within the academic literature to use the term 'capture' in several different
senses within the same work. Marver Bernstein (1955)
provides a case in point. In his discussion of the
"capture" problem he mentions all of the following
conditions: (1) the conscious protection of the interests of the regulated industry (pp. 270-271); (2)
dependence on the utility for information needed for
the performance of the commission's function (pp.
268-269); (3) recruitment of commission personnel from
the ranks of the regulated (pp. 258 ff); and (4) allowing the regulated to take the initiative in shaping
regulatory activity, while either remaining passive
with respect to public needs (pp. 92, 270) or equating
the public good with the good of the utility (p. 269).
The ambiguity resulting from conflating these senses
justifies our explicit distinction among the senses
in which the term 'alignment' will be used in this
study.

Of the eight senses of alignment distinguished
above, only five will be dealt with in the following
discussion. One sense omitted is what might be called
"alignment by diversion" (number (5) above), referring
to all those ways in which a Commission may become em-
broiled in the details of rule and procedure and so
be diverted away from a more substantial concern for
the public interest. This sense of alignment is es-

67

sentially passive: instead of activity on behalf of
the regulated utilities it involves the absence of
activity on behalf of the public, when such activity
would be contrary to utility interests. A peculiar
characteristic of this sort of alignment is that it
tends to escape the awareness of those most afflicted
by it. Insofar as it represents a diversion of attention, one who is aware of its influence is to that
extent undiverted, or in our terms unaligned. Thus
we were not able to measure the extent to which specific individuals in our sample were aligned on this
measure.[1] The other two senses omitted are the last
two listed above (political pressure and undue influence upon individuals), which are difficult to
measure in a study relying almost entirely on data
drawn from individual respondents. The former is
difficult to measure because it is a condition external to the Commission; the latter because a respondent who had succumbed to improper inducement would
not be expected to admit it.[2]

The first of the five types of alignment to be
examined, which we will call "decisional alignment,"
is in some ways the most straightforward. If it were
possible to observe all the relevant decision-behav-
ior of the commissioners and staff, we might simply
identify those decisions made in favor of utility interests at various levels of the regulatory process
and measure decisional alignment in terms of percentages. Unfortunately, we have access to data of the
sort this would require only at the final stage, in
the decisions of the Commissioners themselves. Earlier decisions made by technical staff and by Hearing Examiners--decisions which certainly have some
impact upon the final outcome--are not matters of public record.[3] Another difficulty is that we have no
uniform criteria for identifying decisions made in
the utility's interests. For example, we have no way
of determining whether a regulatory decision which
cuts a proposed rate increases in half ought to count
as a decision contrary to utility interest or not,
since it is possible that the utility's original request was for a rate twice what it actually desired,
so that the decision was effectively favorable to the
utility's cause.

In the present study we have avoided these difficulties by using a kind of surrogate decision-making

68

context. We asked each of the respondents in our
study to complete a questionnaire consisting of
eight hypothetical cases, each pertaining to decision-making in an electric utility company or in
some other industry group or regulatory body. In
each of these hypothetical scenarios a decision had
been made, in most cases one clearly favorable or
unfavorable to the interests of an electric utility
or to the electric power industry as a whole. The
extent to which a respondent agreed with the decisions favorable to the utilities and disagreed with
those which were antithetical became our measure of
"decisional alignment."

For example, one of the scenarios presented a
case in which the Board of Directors of an electric
utility voted to encourage the construction of an
automated steel plant in their service area. The
facts of the case as presented in the scenario stress
that the utility stands to benefit, but that few public benefits and considerable public harm might result from the plant's construction. A respondent who
agreed with the Board's decision would receive one
point on our scale of "decisional alignment," and
would receive two points if he or she strongly a-
greed.[4] A total of fourteen points could be accum-
mulated from all the scenarios contributing to this
measure (results from one of the eight were not us-
able), with seven or more points counting as an indication of alignment.

A second type of alignment involves an explicit
endorsement of utility interests. This type will be
termed "cliental alignment," since it is similar to
Bernstein's notion of "clientalism" (Bernstein, 1955,
pp. 270-271). Our measure of cliental alignment is
a five-point additive scale, with three or more points
counting as a positive indication. One point each
was assigned for (a) explicit reference to utility
interests in the respondent's discussion of the ICC
mandate (questionnaire, p. 21), and (b) for reasoning
emphasizing utility interests on one of the four scenarios (three, four, five and seven) that presented
the clearest distinction among the various interests
in question.

The third type of alignment is present when the
regulator has been an employee of the regulated in-

69

dustry in the past, or has regular informal contact
with utility personnel. Either fact may be sufficient
to label a regulator as being "in the pocket" of the
utility. We will call this type "associational alignment."

"Associational alignment" was measured by a two-
item weighted index consisting of (1) past employment
with a regulated utility (two points) and (2) frequency of informal contact with representatives of
regulated utilities (four points assigned if the contacts are more than weekly, three if they are weekly,
two if monthly, and one if less than monthly). Although arbitrary, the relative weight assigned to
these two variables was intended to be intuitively
plausible and conservative. An individual who has
frequent current contacts on an informal basis with
utility representatives, for example, seems to be
more closely associated than does another who had been
employed by the industry in the past but who has little current contact.

A fourth type of alignment which appears repeat-
edly in the academic literature on regulation is dependence of the regulatory commission upon the regulated industry for information and expertise. This
type will be referred to as "dependency alignment."
Discussions of how regulators can remain independent
in this regard have centered largely around problems
of resources and talent. It has been argued that commission staffs are inevitably overworked and underpaid,
with the result that they rarely have the time or
ability to perform fully independent studies of regulatory issues, being forced instead to rely on the
data and conclusions provided by the utilities themselves.

In the longer of our two questionnaires, the respondents were asked to tell how frequently they had
contact personally with a number of potential information sources, including some utility contacts, and
to estimate the frequency of such contacts for the
Commission as a whole. They were also asked to indicate which of these inputs were of importance to them.
Thus an individual might be considered to be personally dependent on utility sources to the extent that (1)
contacts with such sources are frequent in comparison
to non-utility contacts, or (2) such contact is re-

garded by the respondent as having major importance. One point on a three-point scale was scored for each of these two response patterns. A third point was counted if the respondent frequently supported a hypothetical decision by a utility company on the grounds that "management knows best," as, for example in the following statement: "I have no reason to question the intelligence of management who should have sufficient detailed facts and information available to make an informed judgment."[5] Two or more points were counted as an indication of dependency alignment.

The fifth type of alignment identifiable is the failure of a commission to take initiative on behalf of the public interest because of a restrictive conception of the commission's responsibility and proper role. "Alignment by inertia" (or "inertial alignment") is the name we have given to such failure of initiative.

Some regulators appear restrained in their activity by a "strict constructionist" conception of regulatory activity, and in this manner are inertially aligned with the interests of the regulated utilities. Our seventh scenario was specifically designed to test for a predominantly reactive stance with regard to the proper role of the regulator. Two of three alternative regulatory stances offered for consideration involved a rejection of policies encouraging environmentally innovative action on the part of utilities. A respondent was counted as aligned by this measure if he or she responded to this scenario by favoring either of these two essentially reactive stances.

Measures for these five types of alignment are summarized in Table 3.1, along with the criteria used in each case to identify aligned respondents.

RELATIONSHIPS AMONG THESE TYPES OF ALIGNMENT

Several questions arise regarding the relationships among the types of alignment distinguished in the previous section. First is the question whether they are independent, or whether they are merely different manifestations of the same phenomenon. If the

71

former, then the academic accounts from which these several types were drawn are open to criticism for not recognizing what might be important distinctions. If the latter, then at very least a standardization of terminology would appear to be in order. A second question is whether one or more type (or manifestation) of alignment lead to more critical lapses than others do in the proper performance of the regulatory task. Given an affirmative answer to this, a third question arises whether these others might contribute to the more critical types of alignment, and how such contributions might be expected to occur.

Degree of independence among the types of alignment identified above was tested by determining the product-moment correlation[6] among results of the five alignment measures grouped by pairs. A low correlation (coefficient approaching zero) for a given pair indicates that the two types of alignment concerned are probably independent. A strongly positive correlation (coefficient significantly higher than zero) indicates that the types of alignment concerned are identical or perhaps causally related, or (a possibility to bear in mind) that the measures of alignment employed to indicate the two types contain overlapping or otherwise interacting items. A strongly negative correlation (coefficient significantly less than zero), on the other hand, would indicate that the types of alignment are mutually exclusive, or (possibly) that the measures contain incompatible items.

Results of the independence test are shown in Table 3.2, and schematically in Figure 3.1. With three exceptions, all pairs tested appear independent. One exception is with the strongly positive correlation between associational and dependency alignment. This result is probably due in part to the fact that frequency of contact with utility personnel figured in our measures for both types of alignment, although there is plausibility as well in the reasoning that those regulators most reliant upon the utilities for information are most likely to associate frequently with utility personnel. In either case, this relationship between associational and dependency alignment appears to be of little practical interest, since neither appears to contribute markedly to alignment of any other type.

FIGURE 3.1
Relationships Among Alignment Types

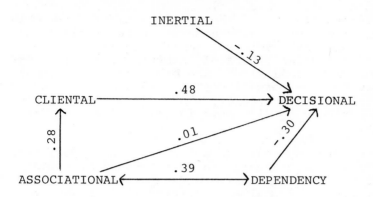

Interpretation of the other two exceptions--
strongly positive correlation between cliental and
decisional alignment, and the strongly negative correlation between decisional and dependency--hangs upon
an answer to the second question posed at the beginning of this section. Whether certain types of alignment contribute more than others to critical lapses
in regulatory performance is a factual question, but
not one that comes within the range of our present
statistical tests. Reflection upon the nature of
these several types of alignment, however, should make
the answer to this question apparent. Since it is not
one of the functions (at least not the primary function) of regulation directly to serve the regulated
industry, a bias in favor of the utility interests
would encourage decisions tending to favor those interests unduly, which in turn would constitute a lapse
in proper regulatory performance. Inasmuch as our
measures of decisional alignment are intended to indicate a propensity to make decisions of this character, the presence of this form of alignment counts as
evidence of such a bias. Moreover, cliental alignment
as we have defined it amounts to an explicit expression of such a bias. These two forms of alignment accordingly would seem to be indicative of the possibility of more critical lapses in regulatory performance
than the three remaining forms. To put it another
way, to the extent that our measures are accurate, decisional alignment amounts to a lapse in proper regu-

latory performance, while cliental alignment amounts
to a propensity to commit such lapses. The strong
correlation found between cliental and decisional
alignment (positive coefficient of .48) corroborates
this interpretation of their interaction. With this
empirical support, the reasoning above warrants our
considering both decisional and cliental alignment
as the most direct forms of "capture" to which a regulator might fall prey. The other types in comparison may be considered indirect, and a significant impediment to the regulatory task only insofar as they
may contribute to alignment in one of the more direct
senses.

Our finding that there is no strongly positive
correlation between any indirect type of alignment
(inertial, associational and dependency) and either
direct type (cliental and decisional) is reason to
conclude that in fact none of the indirect types contribute significantly to alignment of a more critical
nature. Particularly noteworthy is the strongly negative correlation between dependency and decisional
alignment, which indicates that regulators among our
respondents who tend to rely upon the utilities for
information are actually disinclined as a group to
reach decisions favorable to utility interests.

By way of summary, the results of our correlation tests show (1) that several independent forms
of regulatory posture go under the single descriptive
term 'capture' in the academic literature, (2) that
there is a strongly positive correlation between the
two most direct and hence most critical types of
alignment or "capture," and (3) the other less critical and indirect types of alignment do not contribute
markedly to alignment in the forms that make a practical difference, and hence do not constitute a serious
impediment to the regulatory task.

TESTS OF HYPOTHESIS ONE

The first hypothesis posed for test in this study
is that a significant number of regulators with the
ICC are not aligned with the industry they regulate.
In view of the distinction noted above between direct
and indirect forms of alignment, it is appropriate to
tally our results with respect to the former class

separately. It is appropriate further to indicate
results for each of the five types of alignment taken
individually, and for all five types taken as a group.
Data yielding results under these several headings
are reported in Tables 3.3 and 3.4.

Considering all types of alignment together as
a group, we find that only 20 percent of the respondents (six of thirty for which we have at least three
alignment measures--cases 7, 9, 18, 23, 29 and 39 in
Table 3.4) are not aligned in any sense whatever.
Considering each type of alignment individually, on
the other hand, there is only one sense in which more
than approximately one-fourth are aligned--namely the
sense of inertial alignment.[7] Since inertial alignment did not appear positively correlated with either
of the direct forms of alignment, the relatively high
value of 73 percent does not provide reason for sus-
pecting an improper involvement of the ICC with the
industry it regulates. The least auspicious interpretation of this result is that a majority of our
respondents hold conceptions of their own responsibilities which tend to perpetuate the status quo and
hence to discourage new responses to contemporary
regulatory problems.

Our most important finding is that only 27 percent (8 of 30) of our respondents are aligned in the
direct sense of typically making decisions in favor
of the utilities (decisional alignment), and that
none is aligned in the direct sense of explicitly
emphasizing utility interests (cliental alignment).
Conversely, we find that 73 percent are not aligned
in any direct sense. This constitutes definitive
confirmation of our first hypothesis, in the most
relevant sense in which it could plausibly be interpreted. A strong majority of regulators in the ICC
are not aligned with the industry they regulate in a
manner affecting the proper performance of their regulatory task.

NOTES

1. It was possible, however, to examine the
perceptions of the respondents about the extent of
such diversionary alignment in the commission as a
whole. There were two relevant items in our question-

naire:

"Given the present legal and political
structure, the regulatory commission has
relatively little room for discretion in
the decisions it makes," and "It is often hard to get things done because of
the amount of red tape involved [in the
ICC as an organization]."

Thirty-three of 42 respondents (or 79 percent) disagreed with the first statement, suggesting that few
of the respondents see the Commission as diverted because of external legal or political detail. The respondents were about evenly divided (22 agreeing, 20
disagreeing) as to whether internal red tape represents a source of diversion.

2.   A small amount of data were obtained on
these two topics. Responding to a questionnaire item
asking about political pressure as influence upon
their work, 74 percent said it was of little or no
significance in their own case but 79 percent judged
it to be of at least moderate importance to the Commission as a whole. A rough indication of extent of
untoward personal inducement by industry is provided
by the employment records of past commissioners,
briefly summarized in Appendix A.

3.   Although we had access to Commission files,
this source was not helpful here since Commission policy does not require retention of working drafts containing staff recommendations.

4.   Six scenarios (numbers two through seven)
involved choices between the interests of a utility
company and those of some other entity. Because
Scenarios three and five posed the issue in more unambiguous form than the others, responses favoring
the utility on these two were given greater weight
in the scaling,--three points for strong agreement
and two points for agreement.

5.   It appears that this pattern of response represents something more than a reaction to perceived
informational gaps in our scenarios, since it would
have been just as simple for a respondent to decline
to answer in such a case (as some in fact did). We

76

may reasonably assume that those who deferred to managerial wisdom or knowledge in such hypothetical situations did so out of habit, and that such deference is likewise their typical mode of response to analogous situations of informational inadequacy in the real world.

6. The particular correlation measure to be used here is Pearson's r, or the product-moment correlation. Briefly stated, Pearson's r is a measure of the strength and direction of linear association between two variables. It may take values between +1.0 and -1.0, with a value of 0.0 indicating no relationship between the variables in question. What constitutes a "high" or a "low" correlation is to some extent a matter of judgment, but as a general rule we can say that any correlation which would be obtained by chance fewer than five percent of the time may be considered to be statistically significant. The exact size of a significant correlation varies with the size of the sample on which it is based.

7. With regard to dependency alignment, it is worth noting that although individual respondents do not appear heavily dependent upon the regulated industry for information and other inputs, it does seem that many respondents feel this dependence to exist within the Commission at large. Thirty-three of 43 respondents, or 77 percent, agreed with the following statement:

> "Utility company respresentatives generally
> have the advantage over commission staff in
> presenting the facts relating to cases con-
> cerning the electric power industry."

This is a concern which we found mentioned several times in the Commission's own internal management review, and one which has been a perennial problem for regulatory commissions generally.

TABLE 3.1

Summary of Measures Used
for Different Types
of Alignment

Alignment Type	Measure	Criterion for Judging Cases as Being Aligned
Decisional	Pro-utility decisions	Score 50% or more of max. poss. (>7)
Cliental	Pro-utility decisions, with accounts in terms of utility interests	Score 50% or more of max. poss. (>3)
Associational	Past employment by and/ or current informal contact with utility	Score 50% or more of max. poss. (>3)
Dependency	Relative frequency of utility input, felt importance of utility input, and deference to managerial wisdom	Score 50% or more of max. poss. (≥2)
Inertial	Reactive regulatory stance	Rejection of innovative position on scenario 7

78

TABLE 3.2

Product-moment Correlations Among
Five Measures of Alignment

Alignment Types	Decisional	Cliental	Associational	Dependency	Inertial
Decisional		.48***	.01	-.30*	-.13
Cliental			.28	-.12	.11
Associational				.39**	-.11
Dependency					.24
Inertial					

*p<.05   **p<.01   ***p<.005

79

TABLE 3.3

Extent of Alignment of Different Types

Alignment Types and Measures	Total Valid Cases	Highest Possible Score	Highest Actual Score	Mean Score	Number Aligned	Percentage Aligned
Decisional	30	14	9	5.3	8	27
Cliental	30	5	2	0.57	0	0
Associational	40	6	6	1.1	8	20
Dependency	45	3	2	0.6	3	7
Inertial	26	1	1	0.7	19	73

TABLE 3.4

Alignment Status of Individual Respondents
On All Measures of Alignment

Case	Measures of Alignment					Alignment Ratio[1]
	Decisional	Cliental	Associational	Dependency	Inertial	
1	-	-	o	o	-	0/2
2	x	o	o	o	x	2/5
3	-	-	o	o	-	0/2
4	-	-	o	o	-	0/2
5	o	o	o	x	x	2/5
6	o	o	x	o	-	1/4
7	o	o	o	o	o	0/5
8	x	o	x	o	x	3/5
9	o	o	o	o	-	0/4
10	x	o	o	o	o	1/5
11	o	o	o	o	x	1/5
12	o	o	o	o	x	1/5
13	o	o	-	o	x	1/4
14	o	o	o	o	x	1/5
15	-	¡	x	-	-	1/1

[1]Number of scales showing alignment/total number of valid scales.

TABLE 3.4
(Continued)

Case	Measures of Alignment					Alignment Ratio
	Decisional	Cliental	Associational	Dependency	Inertial	
16	-	-	x	x	-	2/2
17	o	o	o	o	x	1/5
18	o	o	o	o	-	0/4
19	x	o	o	o	o	1/5
20	-	-	o	o	-	0/2
21	-	-	o	-	-	0/1
22	o	o	o	o	x	1/5
23	o	o	o	o	o	0/5
24	x	o	o	o	x	2/5
25	-	-	x	-	-	1/1
26	o	o	o	o	x	1/5
27	-	-	x	-	-	1/1
28	x	o	o	o	x	2/5
29	o	o	o	o	o	0/5
30	x	o	o	o	-	1/4
31	o	o	x	o	o	1/5
32	o	o	o	x	x	2/5
33	-	-	o	-	-	0/1

TABLE 3.4
(Continued)

Case	Measures of Alignment					Alignment Ratio
	Decisional	Cliental	Associational	Dependency	Inertial	
34	-	-	-	-	-	-*
35	-	-	o	-	-	0/1
36	o	o	o	o	x	1/5
37	-	-	o	-	-	0/1
38	o	o	o	o	x	1/5
39	o	o	o	o	o	0/5
40	o	o	-	-	x	1/3
41	-	-	o	-	-	0/1
42	o	o	-	-	x	1/3
43	x	o	x	o	x	3/5
44	o	o	o	o	x	1/5
45	-	-	-	-	-	-*

Code: x = aligned
o = nonaligned
- = data missing

*Measures of alignment were totally lacking on these two cases; they have been retained because they did include responses on other items in the study.

4 Alignment and Values

VALUE PATTERNS IN THE ICC

This study of alignment patterns in the ICC has
been guided by the conjecture that the value-orientations of individual regulators contribute to the success or failure of the regulatory task. Failure in
regulation occurs when (but of course not only when)
decisions of the regulatory body give priority to
utility over public interest. Success occurs, on the
other hand, when (among other things) decisions of the
body exhibit a balance giving proper emphasis to the
interests of the public. Commissions tending to give
priority to regulated industry are said, broadly
speaking, to be "captured" by or aligned with the
regulated industry.

To sustain our guiding conjecture it is necessary to show, first, that there are both aligned and
nonaligned regulators within the ICC and, second, that
aligned and nonaligned regulators are characterized
generally by different value-orientations. The first
was shown in the previous chapter. It is the purpose
of the present chapter to test the second specific
hypothesis that aligned and nonaligned regulators have
significantly different value-orientations. Data to
test this hypothesis were gathered by three standardized value instruments: the Allport Study of Values
(1970), the California Life Goals Evaluation Schedule

84

(CLGES; Hahn, 1969), and the Rokeach Value Survey
(1967). Norms have been established for each test
relating to the public at large. Confirmation of the
second hypothesis would consist in showing that
aligned and nonaligned regulators among our respondents differ in their value-orientations, relative to
these established norms. The first step in testing
this hypothesis, accordingly, is to compare the value-
orientations of our respondents as a group with those
of the general population. This is accomplished in
the present section, after which we turn to a comparison between the two classes of regulators.

The Study of Values yields six scores indicating
the relative importance to the individual of six major areas of experience: theoretical, economic, aesthetic, social, political and religious. When the
distribution of test scores for the individual regulators is compared to the distributions that would be
expected from the test norms, no significant difference in the frequency of high and low scores appears
between the regulators and the population at large
(Table 4.1).[1] A comparison of the ICC mean scores on
the six scales with the population norms (Table 4.2),[2]
on the other hand, indicates two noteworthy differences: the ICC respondents scored significantly lower
on both the social and the religious scales.

These indications could be misleading. Allport
has found sharp differences between the sexes in the
rankings assigned to the six areas, and there is a
different proportion of males among the regulators
(about 80 percent) and among the group yielding the
norm (66 percent). The norms for females are significantly higher than those for males on the aesthetic,
social, and religious dimensions, and significantly
lower on the remaining three scales. It thus appears
that separate analyses by sex might yield more reliable results (caution would be required due to the
small number of female respondents--8 of the total 42).
Nonetheless, an examination of the scores on case-
by-case basis shows that the score distribution for
female regulators clearly differs on the political
dimension from the distribution of scores for the female population at large, and appears to differ on the
social and religious dimensions as well (Table 4.3).[3]
A higher proportion of female regulators than would be
expected in the general population exhibit low scores

on the social and religious dimensions and high scores
on the political dimension. This suggests that the
finding of low social and religious scores for the ICC
overall is probably valid, since it is supported even
in those cases (females) where it is least likely to
appear.

This finding also indicates that occupational
context outweighs gender as a determinant of value
orientation within our sample. Accordingly, we will
assume in the remainder of the analysis that there
is no significant sex bias within our sample and that
there is no further need for separate analyses by sex.

The California Life Goals Evaluation Schedules
yield ten scores corresponding to ten personal life
goals, as itemized in Table 4.4. This table shows
the mean scores on these ten scales for the ICC respondents compared with those for the population at
large.[4] The ICC sample scored significantly higher
on the leadership and self-expression scales, and
significantly lower on esteem and social service. The
first three differences are not surprising, since the
regulatory context offers considerable opportunity for
exercising leadership and various other personal tal-
ents, but also exposes the regulator to low public
esteem (Dowling, et al., 1976, p. 1.1). Thus we
might expect persons with these value characteristics
to enter and to remain in the regulatory field. But
the lower mean score on social service is puzzling,
since the work of the regulator would certainly seem
to be of service to society.[5]

The third value test administered to the ICC
respondents was the Rokeach Value Survey. Tables 4.5
and 4.6 present the average (mean) ranks assigned by
the ICC respondents respectively to eighteen "terminal" and eighteen "instrumental" values, compared
with the average ranks obtained by Rokeach in his national sample.[6] There are five "terminal" values in
which the mean rank of the regulators differs significantly from that of the general population. The
regulators as a group assign greater importance to
"inner harmony" and "mature love," and less importance
to "a comfortable life," "a world at peace," and "a
world of beauty." Of these differences in terminal
values, the one that seems most likely to be reflected
in regulatory decision-making is the lower valuation

of personal comfort, suggesting an ability to resist material blandishments of the sort alluded to in some of the academic literature on the perils of regulation. Here we find additional evidence that the "self-interest maximizing" theory of "capture" in particular is not likely to apply to the ICC.

As to instrumental values, the ICC respondents assign greater importance (lower mean ranks) than the general population to being "capable," "logical" and "responsible," and less importance (higher mean ranks) to being "ambitious," "clean," and obedient." Needless to say, emphasis on responsibility and de-emphasis on ambition are not objectionable traits in a regulator.

If we look at the overall pattern, however, it appears that there is more similarity than difference between the rankings given to the two sets of values by the ICC respondents and those given by the population at large. Tables 4.7 and 4.8 list the values in these two sets respectively from most to least important, as indicated by the aggregated rankings by these two groups.[7] A statistically signigicant correlation is present between the two groups for both sets of values (Spearman's rho[8] of .728 for terminal and .492 for instrumental values). Hence it appears that the values of the ICC regulators on the whole are quite similar to those of the general public.

TESTS OF HYPOTHESIS TWO

Among our findings thus far are (1) that alignment is not a unitary phenomenon, but rather includes a number of conditions which appear generally unrelated in the present sample; (2) that most of the regulators in our sample are nonaligned, except in the indirect sense of inertial alignment; and (3) that the regulators exhibit value patterns which generally are similar to those of the public at large. In the present section we proceed directly to test our second hypothesis, that the values of aligned and nonaligned regulators are significantly different.

If alignment were a single characteristic, or if we had found that the several forms of alignment were highly correlated, our present task would have been a

simple one. As matters stand, we must test the hypothesis separately for each type of alignment that
might reasonably be considered associated with value
differences. Of the five types of alignment examined
in this study, four fit that description. Since values (in the relevant sense defined in Chapter Two) are
guides for choice, and since decisional alignment is
a matter of making choices of a particular character,
it follows that the regulator's values might have a
bearing upon whether he or she is aligned in this
fashion. Cliental alignment, in turn, is a matter of
explicit commitment to industry interests. Since
commitments are incentives for action, and hence themselves constitute values (again by the definition in
Chapter Two), cliental alignment might reasonably be
expected to show some association with value orientation. Inertial alignment, furthermore, is a matter
of construing one's obligations as a regulator in a
particular fashion, which again would appear to be a
matter of value orientation. Finally, although asso-
ciating with one or another group of persons does not
itself appear to be an exercise of a particular value
set, it does seem reasonable to expect people to associate with other people with similar values. Thus
values should have some bearing also on associational
alignment. The one type of alignment that seems initially unlikely to show any correlation with particular value patterns is dependency alignment. That a
regulatory commission is dependent upon the regulated
industries for information is simply a matter of fact,
which the individual regulator very likely can do little about. Although he may view this fact as good,
bad or indifferent, dependency alignment itself is not
a matter of values.

This reasoning suggests that we might reasonably
look for value differences between aligned and nonaligned regulators along four alignment dimensions:
decisional, cliental, association, and inertial.
Since no cases of clientally aligned regulators appeared in our sample, however, the second hypothesis
was tested with reference to three types of alignment
--decisional, associational, and inertial.

The strategy chosen was to compare by a standard
difference-of-means technique (called "student's t;"
see footnote 2 of this chapter) the scores registered
by aligned and by nonaligned individuals on the All-

port, CLGES and Rokeach value tests. Data used in
these comparisons are presented in Tables 4.9 through
4.17, and summarized in Tables 4.18 through 4.21.[9]

Contrary to expectations, an examination of the
data in the summary tables shows no general pattern
of differing value orientations between aligned and
nonaligned respondents for any of the three types of
alignment. With exceptions in the case of a few specific values, aligned and nonaligned individuals assigned about the same relative importance and gave
about the same rank ordering to values across the
range covered by the three tests together.

The exceptions, however, are not without interest. Five statistically significant differences appear between those who are decisionally aligned and
those who are not. The aligned place a lower value
on esteem and social service (Table 4.19), and give
a higher priority to national security, honesty and
responsibility (Tables 4.20 and 4.21). Although not
statistically significant, there appear also to be
possible differences in the higher rank assigned to
freedom (Table 4.20) by the decisionally aligned and
in their lesser preference of happiness, friendship
(Table 4.20), cheerfulness and helpfulness (Table
4.21). Although there is no overall pattern of value
difference in this connection, the decisionally
aligned accordingly seem to be characterized by a more
austere and somewhat more "old-fashioned" value orientation than their nonaligned counterparts.

With the inertially aligned, on the other hand,
we find significantly lower preference for things religious (Table 4.18), less weight given to honesty
but more given to helpfulness, politeness and self-
control (Table 4.21), and much less weight given to
mature love (Table 4.20). A possible explanation is
that our measures for inertial alignment stress the
absence of an aggressive of proactive stance on social
issues, with the result that the nonaligned by this measure may be inclined to social activism. In some manifestations at least, social activism is coupled with
emphases upon religion and love.

In the case of associational alignment, however,
the only significant difference between aligned and
nonaligned was the higher value placed by the latter

89

on self-expression (Table 4.19). No interesting explanation seems available for this finding.

INTERPRETATION

The second specific hypothesis posed for testing
in this study is that aligned and nonaligned regulators within the ICC have significantly different value orientations. When this hypothesis was posed prior
to testing, no distinction was explicit between differences in general patterns of value orientation and
differences in value rankings and preferences. What
we had in mind, with all its admitted vagueness, was
"differences in value that could reasonably be expected to affect the proper performance of the regulator's task." While general patterns of value orientation certainly would meet that description, so also
might less pervasive combinations of individual value
differences, insofar as these individual values affect
the regulator's attitudes toward business and society.

When the second hypothesis is construed as pertaining to general patterns of value orientations, it
is clearly disconfirmed. Whereas in the previous
study (Sayre, 1977, pp. 171-176) our instruments disclosed general patterns of value differences between
utlity executives and the population at large, in the
present study they show unambiguously that, with the
ICC at least, the regulators of the utilites not only
are similar in value orientation to the general public
but also are similar among themselves without respect
to alignment.

When the hypothesis is construed as pertaining
to specific value differences, on the other hand, it
is clearly confirmed. With respect to two forms of
alignment there appear statistically significant differences in specific value preferences between aligned
and nonaligned regulators. Of particular interest is
the correlation between decisional alignment and an
emphasis on the conservative values of national security, responsibility and (to a lesser extent) freedom.
Not only is decisional alignment the most direct and
influential among the several forms we have studied,
but also the values correlated with this form of
alignment are closely akin to several of those found
to characterize the utility executive in the previous

study (notably security, leadership and independence; Sayre, 1977, p. 175).

However, caution is in order regarding both results. From the fact that there is no general pattern of value differences between aligned and nonaligned regulators within the ICC it should not be concluded that no patterns of this sort exist within regulatory bodies across the country generally. It is possible that the range of value differences within any given commission is sufficiently narrow not to become evident in a comparative analysis based on small samples within the organization, but that significant differences exist between entire commissions grouped with respect to their alignment posture. Nor should we conclude from the fact that decisionally aligned regulators within the ICC tend to hold more conservative values than their counterparts that similar correlations would be found within other regulatory bodies. It is possible that the correlation we found was due more to Illinois politics or to local hiring practices than to any causal relationship between particular values and particular forms of behavior.

As indicated in the Preface, our study of this particular commission is intended only as a necessary first step of a more comprehensive attempt to understand the influence of values in the regulatory process generally. The pair of results reported in this chapter are best interpreted as reasons for posing two further hypothesis for testing with a much larger group of respondents: (1) that the distinction between alignment and nonalignment is generally independent of any difference in overall pattern of value orientation, and (2) that decisional alignment in particular is correlated generally with particular value preferences indicative of a conservative mentality.

NOTES

1. The test of significance used here was X^2, a measure of the degree to which the observed distribution for a given interest area differs from the distribution expected by chance if the sample were perfectly similar to the larger population. In this case, X^2 values greater than 9.488 would be needed to refect the assumption of merely chance variation. The

X^2 values obtained here were 6.046, 3.367, 5.626, 8.935, 4.839, and 3.866 respectively.

2. A total of 44 respondents completed the *Study of Values*. Two of these failed to indicate their sex, preferring to remain anonymous throughout their survey responses. These two cases were omitted from Table 4.1 above because the determination of high or low scores is dependent on the sex of the respondent. Student's t is a statistical test used in testing hypotheses about the difference of means between samples when one or both of the samples is small and when the variances of the populations from which the samples are drawn are unknown. The computational formulae for testing the significance of t used in the present work are those given by Blalock (1960, pp. 173-176) for use when we cannot assume equal population variances. The sign of t indicates the direction in which the first mean differs from the second; the absolute value is a function of the sample sizes, the difference between the two means, and the sizes of the standard deviation of the means. How large the t score must be to indicate a difference at a particular level of statistical probability depends on the associated degrees of freedom, which in turn vary with the sample sizes and the standard deviations. For example, in Table 4.2, the degrees of freedom for the various pairs are approximately 43, with the associated critical value of t for p < .05 being 1.682. Values smaller than the critical value associated with particular degrees of freedom are considered not to be statistically significant at that level of probability.

3. The expected frequencies for a sample this small are too low to make reliable use of the X^2 statistic. With a slight loss of information, we can collapse categories into low, average, and high, increasing the expected frequencies for each category to tolerable levels. On this basis, the first three values show no significant differences between the ICC sample and the population norms. The X^2 values for the social, political, and religious areas are 2.75, 6.75, and 2.75 respectively, with probabilities of <.3, <.05, and <.3.

4. As in our previous study (Sayre, 1977, pp. 175-177), we have used correction factors to adjust

92

the sample means for negative response bias. The
nature of the scale items and the scoring pattern
can have the effect of lowering the entire range of
scores for respondents who resist cliche-type statements. Since our interest is with the relative size
of the scores, adding a constant to each mean will
not change the response pattern, and it will permit
a more meaningful comparison with other groups. The
correction factors have been calculated in such a way
that the grand mean (means of means) for each sample
is the same as the grand mean for the population
scores.

5. One of the authors of this study has been
examining a possible ideological bias latent in this
particular scale, which would cause otherwise service-
minded respondents to score lower if they were of a
more conservative political bent. Even if this suggestion should prove correct, however, it would not
seem to account for the pattern observed here, since
nothing in our data points to any conservative bias
in the Commission as a whole.

6. There were only four female respondents to
the Rokeach Value Survey. Since Rokeach provides
only sex-segregated norms for the test, and since the
number of female cases is far too small for any meaningful analysis, these four cases have been omitted
here.

7. We have used median ranks as the basis for
the aggregate rankings here, in the interest of con-
sistency with Rokeach's (1973) work. The use of mean
ranks would have given fairly similar results, however.

8. Spearman's rho is a measure of the similarity
or dissimilarity between two sets of rankings. It has
a range from +1.0 (for identical rankings) to -1.0 (for
completely opposite rankings). The absolute magnitude
of rho indicates whether the degree of relationship is
likely to have been obtained merely by chance; the
sign indicates whether the relationship is positive or
negative. The critical values beyond which particular
values of rho may be considered significant are based
on the number of items being ranked. For eighteen
items (as in the Rokeach rankings), absolute values of
rho greater than or equal to .399 are significant at
the .05 level (i.e., the probability is less than .05

93

that a value of this magnitude would be obtained by chance). The critical value for the .01 level of significance for eighteen items is .564 (see Ferguson, p. 414).

9. In these tables, positive values of t indicate that the mean for nonaligned is higher than the mean for aligned respondents, while negative values indicate that the mean score for the nonaligned is lower. It should be noted that data from the Allport and CLGES tests are summated scores, with a higher total score indicating that the value in question is assigned more importance on the average than another value with a lower score. Data from the Rokeach test, on the other hand, come in the form of rankings, with a higher rank order (e.g. tenth place in the ordered set) indicating that the value in question is deemed less important than a value with a lower rank (e.g. second place in the ordered set). In the interpretation which follows, we have included differences which, while not always statistically significant, are sufficiently large to stand out from the rest of the data. Since the number of regulators who scored as aligned on some of the scales was quite small, only very large differences meet the conditions necessary to rule out chance variation (i.e., achieve statistical significance). We suspect that a larger sample would yield more statistically convincing results.

TABLE 4.1

Distribution of Scores on Allport Study of Values,
ICC Respondents Compared with Test Norms

Interest area	Relationship of ICC Scores to Test Norms				
	V. low	Low	Average	High	V. high
Theoretical	6	4	26	5	1
Economic	3	5	21	6	7
Aesthetic	0	8	20	8	6
Social	8	7	22	5	0
Political	2	6	18	9	7
Religious	7	6	21	4	4
Number expected by chance, for sample size (42)	3.8	6.7	21.0	6.7	3.8

TABLE 4.2

Mean Scores on Allport Study of Values,
ICC Respondents Compared with Test Norms

Interest area	ICC (n=44)		Norm (n=3778)		Difference-of-means test (t)
	X	s	X	s	
Theoretical	40.68	9.30	39.75	7.27	0.66
Economic	42.50	11.96	40.33	7.61	1.19
Aesthetic	38.09	10.31	38.88	8.42	-0.50
Social	35.25	10.34	39.56	7.03	-2.73***
Political	42.30	9.92	40.39	6.44	1.26
Religious	36.66	11.31	41.01	9.31	-2.51**

**p < .01
***p < .005

95

TABLE 4.3

Distribution of Scores on Allport Study of Values,
ICC Female Respondents Compared with Tests Norms
for Females

Interest area	Relationship of ICC Scores to Test Norms				
	V. low	Low	Average	High	V. high
Theoretical	1	1	3	2	1
Economic	0	2	3	2	1
Aesthetic	0	1	5	0	2
Social	3	1	3	1	0
Political	0	0	3	1	4
Religious	2	1	5	0	0
Number expected by chance, for sample size (8)	0.7	1.3	4.0	1.3	0.7

TABLE 4.4

Adjusted Mean Scores and Standard Deviations for
the CLGES, ICC Respondents Compared with
Population Norms

Value	ICC (n=43)		Norms[a] (n=1159)		ICC vs. Norm
	Mean rank	Std. dev.	Mean rank	Std. dev.	
Esteem	29.2	7.1	35.0	8.1	-5.17***
Profit	30.7	7.7	30.0	7.8	0.58
Fame	22.5	5.7	21.0	10.2	1.61
Power	23.2	5.7	22.0	9.8	1.35
Leadership	35.2	7.4	33.0	8.1	1.89*
Security	27.2	6.2	28.0	8.9	-0.81
Social service	26.0	7.4	28.0	10.0	-1.70*
Interest. exp.	32.4	7.4	32.0	7.4	0.34
Self-express.	33.7	6.8	31.0	7.9	2.51**
Independence	29.3	6.6	29.0	7.7	0.29
Correction factor[4]	+3.4		0.0		

*p < .05
**p < .01
***p < .001

[a]Hahn, 1969a, p. 6

TABLE 4.5

Mean Ranks on Rokeach Terminal Values,
ICC Compared with Norms, Males Only[6]

Value	ICC (n=21)		Norms[a] (n=665)		Difference-of-means tests (Student's t)
	Mean rank	Std. dev.	Mean rank	Std. dev.	
Comfortable life	10.91	4.66	8.24	5.16	2.52**
Exciting life	12.24	5.18	13.04	4.75	-0.68
Sense of accomplishment	7.62	4.35	8.73	4.61	-1.12
World at peace	9.00	5.68	5.62	4.75	2.63**
World of beauty	14.29	3.85	12.66	4.32	1.86*
Equality	10.14	5.29	9.28	5.16	0.72
Family Security	6.29	4.05	5.03	3.92	1.37
Freedom	6.24	3.91	5.88	3.94	0.14
Happiness	6.62	4.04	7.97	3.44	-1.48
Inner harmony	7.24	4.46	10.76	4.24	-3.48***
Mature love	10.19	3.91	11.81	4.48	-1.82*
National security	11.38	5.85	9.41	4.78	1.49
Pleasure	12.95	4.12	13.19	3.97	-0.26
Salvation	9.71	6.72	9.48	6.20	0.15
Self-respect	7.14	4.18	8.48	4.28	-1.41
Social recognition	12.86	3.40	13.03	3.95	-0.22
True friendship	10.48	3.01	9.62	4.18	1.24
Wisdom	7.24	5.54	8.78	4.82	-1.23

[a]From Rokeach, 1973, pp. 364-365; higher mean ranks indicate lower priorities.
*p < .05   **p < .01   ***p < .005

TABLE 4.6

Mean Ranks on Rokeach Instrumental Values,
ICC Compared with Norms, Males Only

Value	ICC (n=21) Mean rank	Std. dev.	National sample (n=665) Mean rank	Std. dev.	Difference-of-means tests (Student's t)
Ambitious	10.18	5.23	6.87	5.21	2.79**
Broadminded	9.23	3.94	7.93	5.15	1.44
Capable	6.36	3.13	8.80	4.48	-3.38***
Cheerful	11.41	4.73	10.19	4.73	1.14
Clean	14.41	3.96	9.50	5.03	5.41****
Courageous	9.32	4.15	8.15	4.74	1.24
Forgiving	10.00	5.12	8.59	4.79	1.22
Helpful	9.36	4.27	8.77	4.68	0.61
Honest	3.86	3.85	4.55	3.70	-0.79
Imaginative	13.00	3.99	13.01	4.62	-0.01
Independent	8.23	5.10	9.70	5.12	-1.27
Intellectual	10.50	5.73	11.84	4.77	-1.04
Logical	7.96	3.44	12.34	4.74	-5.54****
Loving	10.09	5.82	10.48	4.89	-0.30
Obedient	14.73	3.12	12.51	4.51	3.09
Polite	10.68	3.91	10.79	4.44	-0.12
Responsible	3.14	2.19	7.18	4.62	-7.75****
Self-controlled	8.55	4.69	9.78	4.85	-1.15

**p < .01   ***p < .005   ****p < .0005

TABLE 4.7

Rank Ordering of Rokeach's Terminal Values
ICC Males Compared with Males in
National Sample

ICC		National sample[a]	
Wisdom	(4.38)[b]	World at peace	(3.75)
Freedom	(5.75)	Family security	(3.86)
Family security	(6.00)[c]	Freedom	(4.91)
Happiness	(6.00)	Comfortable life	(7.77)
Self-respect	(6.33)[c]	Happiness	(7.94)
Sense of accomplishment	(6.33)	Self-respect	(8.16)
Inner harmony	(7.63)	Sense of accomplishment	(8.29)
World at peace	(8.25)	Wisdom	(8.49)
Equality	(10.00)	Equality	(8.87)
True friendship	(10.08)	National security	(9.21)
Mature love	(10.25)	True friendship	(9.63)
Salvation	(11.25)	Salvation	(9.88)
Comfortable life	(11.75)	Inner harmony	(11.08)
National security	(12.75)	Mature love	(12.57)
Exciting life	(13.33)	World of beauty	(13.61)
Social recognition	(14.00)	Social recognition	(13.79)
Pleasure	(14.60)	Pleasure	(14.14)
World of beauty	(15.33)	Exciting life	(14.62)

[a]Based on data in Rokeach, 1973, pp. 57 and 364-465.
[b]Figures in parentheses are median rankings.
[c]In cases where medians were identical, mean rankings were used to determine the relative order of the tied items.

TABLE 4.8

Rank Ordering of Rokeach's Instrumental Values,
ICC Males Compared with Males in National Sample

ICC		National sample[a]	
Honest	(1.50)[b]	Honest	(3.43)
Responsible	(2.50)	Ambitious	(5.61)
Capable	(5.70)	Responsible	(6.58)
Independent	(7.00)	Broadminded	(7.20)
Loving	(8.50)	Courageous	(7.49)
Logical	(8.75)	Forgiving	(8.23)
Broadminded	(9.17)[c]	Helpful	(8.35)
Courageous	(9.17)[c]	Capable	(8.86)
Self-controlled	(9.50)[c]	Clean	(9.43)
Helpful	(9.50)	Self-controlled	(9.65)
Forgiving	(9.50)	Independent	(10.17)
Ambitious	(10.00)[c]	Cheerful	(10.41)
Intellectual	(11.00)[c]	Polite	(10.85)
Polite	(11.00)	Loving	(10.90)
Cheerful	(12.00)	Intellectual	(12.77)
Imaginative	(14.00)	Logical	(13.51)[c]
Clean	(15.50)	Obedient	(13.51)
Obedient	(15.50)	Imaginative	(14.28)

[a]Based on data in Rokeach, 1973, pp. 58 and 366-367.
[b]Figures in parentheses are median rankings.
[c]In cases where medians were identical, mean rankings were used to determine the relative orders of the tied items.

TABLE 4.9

Mean Scores of Aligned and Nonaligned Regulators
on Study of Values and CLGES:
Decisional Alignment

Value	Nonaligned		Aligned		Difference-of-
	Mean rank	Std. dev.	Mean rank	Std. dev.	means tests (Student's t)
Study of Values	(n=21)		(n=8)		
Theoretical	41.43	7.19	44.00	4.18	-0.95
Economic	42.76	9.75	43.00	10.43	-0.06
Aesthetic	39.33	9.27	35.38	6.28	1.11
Social	35.86	6.11	35.00	5.81	0.34
Political	43.33	8.33	45.13	5.94	-0.55
Religious	36.81	10.60	37.63	6.89	-0.20
CLGES	(n=20)		(n=8)		
Esteem	27.85	6.15	23.00	2.62	2.93**
Profit	28.85	6.96	28.00	6.74	0.29
Fame	20.05	4.74	17.63	3.93	1.28
Power	20.90	6.01	19.75	2.32	0.73
Leadership	33.70	6.18	31.88	2.75	1.08
Security	25.85	5.81	21.88	3.40	1.80
Social service	24.65	7.48	17.75	5.34	2.37*
Interest. exp.	28.75	6.47	28.88	5.33	-0.05
Self-express.	30.65	4.13	29.75	5.90	0.46
Independence	27.60	5.45	26.50	4.11	0.51

*p < .05
**p < .01

TABLE 4.10

Mean Ranks Assigned to Terminal Values on Rokeach Value Survey by Nonaligned and Aligned Regulators: Decisional Alignment

Value	Nonaligned (n=19)		Aligned (n=8)		Difference-of-means tests (Student's t)
	Mean rank	Std. dev.	Mean rank	Std. dev.	
Comfortable life	11.21	4.87	12.38	3.58	-0.61
Exciting life	11.47	5.68	11.63	4.98	-0.07
Sense of accomplishment	7.16	4.75	7.50	2.56	-0.19
World at peace	9.42	5.18	9.38	5.71	0.02
World of beauty	13.00	4.40	14.88	2.10	-1.50
Equality	10.47	5.65	9.13	4.70	0.59
Family security	6.53	4.70	7.13	3.09	-0.33
Freedom	6.89	3.73	4.00	3.70	1.85
Happiness	6.42	3.52	9.63	5.50	-1.82
Harmony	7.26	4.09	7.63	4.96	-0.20
Mature love	9.32	4.31	11.50	3.67	-1.25
National security	13.32	4.46	9.00	6.41	2.01*
Pleasure	12.32	4.55	14.75	2.71	-1.40
Salvation	10.32	6.91	9.13	7.10	0.41
Self-respect	7.11	4.22	5.88	4.36	0.69
Social recognition	12.58	3.99	12.75	2.96	-0.11
True friendship	9.37	2.33	11.50	3.38	-1.69
Wisdom	6.89	5.25	7.13	5.41	-0.10

*p < .05

TABLE 4.11

Mean Ranks Assigned to Instrumental Values on Rokeach
Value Survey by Nonaligned and Aligned Regulators:
Decisional Alignment

Value	Nonaligned (n=19)		Aligned (n=8)		Difference-of-means tests (Student's t)
	Mean rank	Std. dev.	Mean rank	Std. dev.	
Ambitious	9.30	5.16	10.25	4.68	-0.45
Broadminded	8.75	4.61	7.75	3.37	0.55
Capable	7.15	4.27	5.88	2.10	0.80
Cheerful	10.25	4.61	13.25	3.73	-1.63
Clean	14.10	4.09	16.00	2.07	-1.24
Courageous	9.15	4.97	8.00	4.41	0.57
Forgiving	10.65	5.05	10.25	5.06	0.19
Helpful	9.00	4.43	11.63	2.56	-1.57
Honest	4.85	3.82	2.00	1.41	2.88**
Imaginative	11.95	4.86	12.13	4.39	-0.09
Independent	7.75	4.94	8.00	5.21	-0.12
Intelligent	10.15	5.79	8.50	5.73	0.69
Logical	8.75	3.52	8.13	3.80	0.42
Loving	10.05	5.51	9.13	5.49	0.40
Obedient	15.00	2.94	15.50	3.12	-0.40
Polite	10.70	4.45	12.25	2.71	-0.91
Responsible	4.20	2.75	2.25	0.71	2.94**
Self-controlled	9.25	5.22	10.13	3.72	-0.43

**p < .01

TABLE 4.12

Mean Scores of Aligned and Nonaligned Regulators
on Study of Values and CLGES:
Associational Alignment

Value	Nonaligned		Aligned		Difference-of-
	Mean rank	Std. dev.	Mean rank	Std. dev.	means tests (Student's t)
Study of Values	(n=32)		(n=7)		
Theoretical	41.31	7.09	40.71	7.54	0.20
Economic	43.13	10.83	46.71	4.23	-1.44
Aesthetic	38.66	9.33	36.86	5.05	0.49
Social	34.84	6.23	35.00	7.70	-0.06
Political	43.94	8.03	43.86	5.87	0.02
Religious	37.84	10.84	36.86	3.72	0.42
CLGES	(n=31)		(n=7)		
Esteem	26.74	6.27	25.86	6.15	0.34
Profit	28.16	6.38	29.14	7.97	-0.35
Fame	19.87	4.55	19.57	7.12	0.14
Power	20.23	5.31	20.29	3.77	-0.03
Leadership	33.10	5.70	30.43	5.97	1.11
Security	24.71	5.28	21.14	3.49	1.70
Social service	22.97	6.94	22.00	4.44	0.35
Interest. exp.	30.32	5.95	29.71	4.61	0.25
Self-express.	31.81	5.43	28.14	2.04	2.95**
Independence	26.81	5.12	25.71	6.42	0.42

**p < .01

105

TABLE 4.13

Mean Ranks Assigned to Terminal Values on Rokeach
Value Survey by Nonaligned and Aligned Regulators:
Associational Alignment

Value	Nonaligned (n=22)		Aligned (n=3)		Difference-of-means tests (Student's t)
	Mean rank	Std. dev.	Mean rank	Std. dev.	
Comfortable life	11.67	4.41	9.33	6.66	0.81
Exciting life	10.67	5.52	13.33	5.51	-0.78
Sense of accomplishment	8.05	4.23	5.67	3.79	0.92
World at peace	9.48	5.10	8.33	8.08	0.34
World of beauty	13.71	4.24	14.33	1.53	-0.25
Equality	9.71	5.42	10.33	6.66	-0.18
Family Security	6.52	4.02	7.00	1.73	-0.20
Freedom	5.90	4.09	5.33	3.79	0.23
Happiness	8.00	4.52	6.00	4.58	0.72
Harmony	6.95	4.66	8.67	1.16	-0.63
Mature love	10.29	4.14	10.67	5.86	-0.14
National security	11.24	5.60	15.00	5.20	-1.09
Pleasure	13.48	4.09	12.67	4.73	0.32
Salvation	9.19	7.03	10.33	8.08	-0.26
Self-respect	6.48	3.98	6.67	6.69	-0.07
Social recognition	12.95	3.72	12.67	2.31	0.13
True friendship	10.10	3.19	11.33	1.16	-0.65
Wisdom	7.81	5.30	6.67	4.73	0.66

TABLE 4.14

Mean Ranks Assigned to Instrumental Values on Rokeach
Value Survey by Nonaligned and Aligned Regulators:
Associational Alignment

Value	Nonaligned (n=22)		Aligned (n=3)		Difference-of-means tests (Student's t)
	Mean rank	Std. dev.	Mean rank	Std. dev.	
Ambitious	9.32	4.97	14.67	3.51	-1.79
Broadminded	8.55	4.49	7.33	3.79	0.44
Capable	6.55	4.21	8.33	1.53	-0.72
Cheerful	10.55	4.87	14.00	1.73	-1.20
Clean	14.59	3.96	15.00	2.65	-0.17
Courageous	7.91	4.57	9.33	4.51	-0.51
Forgiving	10.91	4.68	6.33	2.89	1.63
Helpful	9.82	3.96	10.33	4.51	-0.21
Honest	3.91	3.48	1.00	0.00	1.42
Imaginative	12.45	4.46	10.33	5.69	0.75
Independent	8.23	4.87	7.33	3.22	0.31
Intelligent	10.36	5.39	11.00	7.94	-0.18
Logical	8.45	3.66	8.33	3.06	0.05
Loving	10.18	5.51	4.67	1.16	1.70
Obedient	14.77	3.16	17.00	1.00	-1.19
Polite	11.27	4.14	13.33	2.31	-0.83
Responsible	3.68	2.75	2.33	0.58	0.83
Self-controlled	9.50	4.91	10.33	5.77	-0.27

TABLE 4.15

Mean Scores of Aligned and Nonaligned Regulators
on Study of Values and CLGES:
Inertial Alignment

Value	Nonaligned		Aligned		Difference-of-
	Mean rank	Std. dev.	Mean rank	Std. dev.	means tests (Student's t)
Study of Values	(n=7)		(n=18)		
Theoretical	37.57	8.58	43.56	5.18	-1.61
Economic	39.14	11.34	44.33	10.09	-0.99
Aesthetic	40.57	10.80	37.89	8.76	0.55
Social	34.57	6.63	35.89	6.46	-0.42
Political	46.29	6.87	43.44	8.09	0.83
Religious	41.86	7.84	34.39	9.98	1.86*
CLGES	(n=7)		(n=17)		
Esteem	28.80	8.16	28.80	5.00	0.00
Profit	31.80	7.02	32.20	7.03	-0.12
Fame	21.50	6.53	21.70	3.04	-0.07
Power	24.10	4.50	23.00	5.97	0.46
Leadership	34.10	7.09	36.90	4.79	-0.89
Security	26.90	5.83	27.70	5.62	-0.29
Social service	24.80	5.28	25.00	8.63	-0.07
Interest. exp.	33.90	6.40	31.00	6.57	0.94
Self-express.	32.20	3.64	33.60	5.30	-0.70
Independence	30.60	6.87	29.60	4.54	0.33

*p < .05

TABLE 4.16

Mean Ranks Assigned to Terminal Values on Rokeach
Value Survey by Nonaligned and Aligned Regulators:
Inertial Alignment

Value	Nonaligned (n=6)		Aligned (n=18)		Difference-of-means tests (Student's t)
	Mean rank	Std. dev.	Mean rank	Std. dev.	
Comfortable life	12.83	5.04	11.44	4.49	0.56
Exciting life	9.50	6.54	11.39	5.11	-0.59
Sense of accomplishment	6.67	2.34	8.11	4.60	-0.94
World at peace	12.00	3.41	8.78	5.43	1.60
World of beauty	13.83	3.66	12.94	4.15	0.46
Equality	11.50	6.12	9.33	5.48	0.71
Family security	6.83	3.17	6.83	4.81	0.00
Freedom	7.17	5.49	5.72	3.53	0.56
Happiness	7.33	5.32	8.00	4.16	-0.26
Harmony	5.50	3.02	8.33	4.54	-1.62
Mature love	6.17	1.84	11.50	3.97	-4.21****
National security	12.50	6.09	11.33	5.39	0.39
Pleasure	14.17	3.31	12.67	4.54	0.81
Salvation	7.33	7.17	11.22	6.77	-1.08
Self-respect	4.50	2.81	7.33	4.46	-1.71
Social recognition	14.33	3.20	11.72	3.83	1.53
True friendship	9.33	3.56	10.22	3.28	-0.50
Wisdom	9.17	4.79	5.83	5.27	1.34

****p < .0005

TABLE 4.17

Mean Ranks Assigned to Instrumental Values on Rokeach
Value Survey by Nonaligned and Aligned Regulators:
Inertial Alignment

Value	Nonaligned (n=6)		Aligned (n=18)		Difference-of-means tests (Student's t)
	Mean rank	Std. dev.	Mean rank	Std. dev.	
Ambitious	7.33	5.24	9.16	4.34	-0.71
Broadminded	9.17	4.75	8.79	4.22	0.16
Capable	5.33	5.82	6.74	2.81	-0.52
Cheerful	10.33	5.01	11.37	4.76	-0.41
Clean	15.00	2.83	15.00	3.15	0.00
Courageous	6.00	4.05	9.68	5.06	-1.68
Forgiving	11.33	4.13	10.37	5.58	-0.42
Helpful	12.50	2.67	9.21	4.40	2.05*
Honest	2.33	1.97	4.90	3.86	-2.00*
Imaginative	11.33	5.09	11.74	4.84	-0.16
Independent	7.83	4.83	7.68	5.09	0.06
Intelligent	7.17	2.99	10.00	5.92	-1.44
Logical	8.17	3.31	8.79	3.85	-0.35
Loving	9.00	5.76	10.47	5.54	-0.51
Obedient	16.17	2.40	14.68	3.25	1.12
Polite	13.67	2.50	10.32	4.14	2.23*
Responsible	5.17	3.87	3.32	1.92	1.03
Self-controlled	13.17	2.56	8.79	4.89	2.66**

*p < .05   **p < .01

TABLE 4.18

Summary of Difference-of-Means Tests Results (Student's t)
Comparing Nonaligned and Aligned Regulators in the Allport
Study of Values, for Different Measures of Alignment

Value	Measures of Alignment		
	Decisional	Associational	Inertial
Theoretical	-0.95	0.20	-1.61
Economic	-0.06	-1.44	-0.99
Aesthetic	1.11	0.49	0.55
Social	0.34	-0.06	-0.42
Political	-0.55	0.02	0.83
Religious	-0.20	0.42	1.86*
Number of nonaligned	21	32	7
Number of aligned	8	7	18

*p < .05

TABLE 4.19

Summary of Difference-of-Means Tests Results (Student's t)
Comparing Nonaligned and Aligned Regulators in the
California Life Goals Evaluation Schedules
for Different Measures of Alignment

Value	Measures of Alignment		
	Decisional	Associational	Inertial
Esteem	2.93**	0.34	0.00
Profit	0.29	-0.35	-0.12
Fame	1.28	0.14	-0.07
Power	0.73	-0.03	0.46
Leadership	1.08	1.11	-0.89
Security	1.80	1.70	-0.29
Social service	2.37*	0.35	-0.07
Interest. exp.	-0.05	0.25	0.94
Self-express.	0.46	2.95**	-0.70
Independence	0.51	0.42	0.33
Number of nonaligned	20	31	7
Number of aligned	8	7	17

*p < .05
**p < .01

112

TABLE 4.20

Summary of Difference-of-Means Tests Results (Student's t)
Comparing Nonaligned and Aligned Regulators in the
Rokeach Value Survey, Terminal Values
for Different Measures of Alignment

Measures of Alignment

Value	Decisional	Associational	Inertial
Comfortable life	-0.61	0.81	0.56
Exciting life	-0.07	-0.78	-0.59
Sense of accomplishment	-0.19	0.92	-0.94
World at peace	0.02	0.34	1.60
World of beauty	-1.50	-0.25	0.46
Equality	0.59	-0.18	0.71
Family security	-0.33	-0.20	0.00
Freedom	1.85	0.23	0.56
Happiness	-1.82	0.72	-0.26
Inner harmony	-0.20	-0.63	-1.62
Mature love	-1.25	-0.14	-4.21****
National security	2.01*	-1.09	0.39
Pleasure	-1.40	0.32	0.81
Salvation	0.41	-0.26	-1.08
Self-respect	0.69	-0.07	-1.71
Social recognition	-0.11	0.13	1.53
True friendship	-1.69	-0.65	-0.50
Wisdom	-0.10	0.66	1.34

*p < .05   ****p < .0005

113

TABLE 4.21

Summary of Difference-of-Means Tests Results (Student's t)
Comparing Nonaligned and Aligned Regulators in the
Rokeach Value Survey, Instrumental Values
for Different Measures of Alignment

Value	Measures of Alignment		
	Decisional	Associational	Inertial
Ambitious	-0.45	-1.79	-0.71
Broadminded	0.55	0.44	0.16
Capable	0.80	-0.72	-0.52
Cheerful	-1.63	-1.20	-0.41
Clean	-1.24	-0.17	0.00
Courageous	0.57	-0.51	-1.68
Forgiving	0.19	1.63	0.42
Helpful	-1.57	-0.21	2.05*
Honest	2.88**	1.42	-2.00*
Imaginative	-0.09	0.75	-0.16
Independent	-0.12	0.31	0.06
Intelligent	0.68	-0.18	-1.44
Logical	0.42	0.05	-0.35
Loving	0.40	1.70	-0.51
Obedient	-0.40	-1.19	1.12
Polite	-0.91	-0.83	2.23*
Responsible	2.94**	0.83	1.03
Self-controlled	-0.43	-0.27	2.66**

*p < .05   **p < .01   ***p < .001

5 Alignment and the Public Interest

THE IMPORTANCE OF HYPOTHESIS THREE

As the reader will recall, this study is premised upon the general hypothesis that the values held by individual members of a regulatory commission affect the performance of the commission overall. Plausible as this hypothesis appears in general form, the role of values in the regulatory process has been uniformly overlooked by academic theorists of regulatory "capture." A secondary goal of the study, accordingly, has been a critical assessment of academic literature on government regulation. If individual values are an important factor in the regulatory process, then no theory of regulation which leaves this factor out of account can be satisfactory in the final analysis. A detailed account of this rationale was given in Chapter One.

To test our general hypothesis we secured the cooperation of the Illinois Commerce Commission--a regulatory body enjoying high repute for value consciousness--and administered instruments for measuring values to 45 of its members. On the basis of data thus obtained, we undertook to test three specific hypotheses projected with reference to that particular group (Chapter Two). First was the hypothesis that a significant number of respondents within the ICC would be found not to be aligned ("captured") by the industries

115

they regulate. For an adequate report of results in
this connection, it was necessary to distinguish between direct forms of alignment, in which the regulator appears given to patterns of thought and action
unduly supportive of utility interest, and indirect
forms over which the individual regulator may have no
personal control and which in themselves are neutral
with respect to the utilities. Our primary concern
was with the former, not only because they are more
substantial in their effect but also because they seem
more likely to be influenced by individual values.

Our finding in connection with the first hypothesis (Chapter Three) was that, whereas 73 percent of
the ICC sample are aligned in some sense or another,
only 27 percent are aligned in the more direct and
practically significant senses. In its most meaningful form, Hypothesis One is confirmed.

The second specific hypothesis was that a significant difference in value orientation is present between aligned and nonaligned regulators within the
ICC. Findings in this regard were reported (in Chapter Four) under two headings. On the one hand, no
broad difference in value-orientation was found either
between the regulators as a group and the general population or between different subgroups among the regulators themselves. In this respect, the second hypothesis was disconfirmed. On the other hand, decisionally aligned and nonaligned regulators were found
to differ significantly in their emphasis on several
particular values that appear germane to the regulatory task. Since decisional alignment is the most
central form treated in the present study, this latter
result constitutes confirmation of the second hypothesis in a limited but important respect. Whether correlations between this form of alignment and these
particular value differences exist across the population of regulators at large, and not just within the
ICC, is a possibility to be studied with a wider group
of respondents.

Third among our specific hypotheses is that nonaligned regulators within the ICC hold conceptions of
the public interest that are ethically distinguishable
from those held by aligned respondents. In order to
avoid begging questions about what values in fact promote the public interest, a matter upon which political

116

and moral theorists have differed for millenia, we have divided this third topic into two parts for empirical testing. First, we have asked whether aligned and nonaligned regulators hold differing conceptions of the public interest they are mandated to protect. Given an affirmative answer to this empirical question, our second concern then would be with whether these conceptions can appropriately and profitably be criticized in light of generally accepted tenets of ethical theory. Findings responding to the first of these queries are reported in the present chapter. For reasons soon to become apparent, the second query is addressed separately in the chapter following.

CONCEPTIONS OF THE PUBLIC INTEREST

The expression 'public interest' admits a wide variety of interpretations. Conceptions of the public interest can be compared with respect to the answers they dictate to the following three questions: (1) who constitutes the public whose interests are being considered?; (2) what policies best serve the interests of this public?; and (3) by what means are these policies best implemented or pursued? The conjecture to be tested by this information is that aligned and nonaligned regulators hold different conceptions of the public interest. Our procedure in testing this conjecture was to compare answers given by aligned and nonaligned respondents to questionnaire items bearing on these three issues. As in the tests of the second hypothesis in the preceding chapter, our concern was limited to three forms of alignment-- decisional, associational and inertial--with each form of alignment considered separately.

To determine whether aligned and nonaligned persons differ in their views about who belongs to the public they serve, we compared their responses to three issues regarding the composition of that public. First was the issue whether the public is a monolithic entity, or instead is composed of multiple constituencies that should be distinguished for regulatory purposes. Our finding was that virtually all regulators, aligned and nonaligned alike, for all forms of alignment, view the public as multidimensional. As Table 5.1(a) indicates,[1] almost all of the respondents consider industry management as being responsible not only

117

to stockholders but to "many constituencies (e.g.,
employees, customers, the public at large)." Since
virtually all respondents agreed unproblematically
that their function is to regulate the industries
concerned in pursuit of this responsibility, it follows that aligned and nonaligned regulators across
the board view the public as being composed of various constituencies. Our second question regarding
the composition of the public was whether special
groups like the poor have standing in their own right
as distinct constituencies. Again a strong consensus
appeared: few regulators view themselves as having
any specific responsibilities to the poor as such
(see Table 5.1(b)). No distinction appears with respect to alignment, for any of the three types of
alignment tested.

Third, we looked for differences between aligned
and nonaligned regulators regarding the status of future generations in the public they serve. Here, too,
the classification of respondents as aligned or nonaligned carries with it no difference in pattern of
response. Without regard to type of alignment, the
aligned and nonaligned regulators all tend to include
future generations among the public to which they are
obligated (Table 5.1(c)). What is not clear is just
how far into the future this obligation is assumed to
extend. When asked in another part of the questionnaire to specify in terms of years what the phrase
"long range" means to them, most respondents indicated
time spans that were surpisingly short. With the
sole exception of the inertially aligned, the median
time span for all subgroups was only ten years; the
median for the inertially aligned was a mere 7.5.
These time spans do not cover a single generation,
and are short even in comparison with responses given
to the same question by the utility executives sur-
veyed in the previous study (Sayre, 1977, p. 258).

Such ambiguity aside, it is clear that alignment
is not a factor in determining a regulator's conception of the composition of the public served. To the
contrary, there is a strong consensus within the Commission that the public is multidimensional, that it
allows no special status to low income members, and
that it includes future generations at least in principle.

118

Agreement regarding the composition of the public does not dictate agreement about policies most likely to serve the public interest. To test for possible differences between aligned and nonaligned respondents in this latter regard, we looked to several questionnaire items concerning policy preferences on such topics as quality of life, growth in energy use, the environment, and solar and nuclear power. Table 5.2 compares the responses to these items of aligned and nonaligned regulators, distinguished according to alignment type. Contrary to expectations based on the third hypothesis, no consistent difference appeared with respect to any type of alignment. On several items there is consensus across the entire group of respondents, and in most cases when consensus is lacking the pattern of divergence is independent of alignment status.

Most respondents agree that progress should be defined in terms of improved quality of life, rather than in terms of gross national product (Table 5.2(a)). Moreover, quality of life is conceived as including material comforts, as indicated by majority agreement with an item suggesting that air conditioning is essential for a moderate standard of living (Table 5.2 (b)).

On the subject of energy use, a majority of both aligned and nonaligned respondents agreed that the nation must move toward lower levels of energy consumption in general (Table 5.2(c)), and must decelerate its growth rate of electric power consumption in particular (Tables 5.2(d) and(e)). A small minority endorsed a policy of zero growth or decrease in electric power use (Table 5.2(f)), and a comparably small minority favored continued growth at present rates or faster (Table 5.2(g)).

The most notable difference between aligned and nonaligned regulators in regard to energy use is that the inertially aligned appear much more inclined to endorse continued growth in electric power use (Table 5.2(g)). This same group is likewise more willing to agree with the notion that air conditioning is a virtual necessity for a moderate standard of living (Table 5.2(b)).

With respect to environment, only about one-third

119

of all our respondents agreed with a statement calling
for less attention in the future to environmental matters, with no significant distinction in response by
alignment type (Table 5.2(b)). This generally favorable attitude toward environmental concerns is sus-
tained in responses to another questionnaire item proposing that the National Environmental Policy Act be
repealed. The approximately one-third agreement with
this proposal showed no correlation with type of
alignment (Table 5.2(i)).

Several items on the questionnaire dealt with
views on nuclear and solar power options. The regulators appear about equally divided overall on the
issue whether nuclear power is "currently the safest
and most practical answer to our nation's energy
needs" (Table 5.2(j)). Although decisionally aligned
and associationally nonaligned appear somewhat more
favorable to the nuclear option than their opposite
numbers, the sample sizes are too small to permit
reliable inferences. Regardless of whether nuclear
power is considered the safest and most practical
answer to our energy needs, a majority of respondents
do favor continued construction of nuclear plants as
part of the state's base load capacity (Table 5.2(k)).
This pattern holds across all types of alignment, for
both aligned and nonaligned respondents. Along with
this general endorsement of nuclear power, however,
we find a majority also agreeing that "the ICC should
actively encourage the use of solar energy within its
jurisdiction." Again, this pattern of positive response holds up across all alignment categories.

Our conclusion with respect to possible policy
differences between aligned and nonaligned regulators
is that, with few exceptions, alignment makes no difference in the regulators' choice of policies which
they believe to be best suited to the public welfare.

Of the three questions concerning the regulators'
conception of the public interest posed at the beginning of this chapter, (Who is the public?, What policies are in the public interest?, How should these
policies be established?), the most informative for
our purposes is the question of means. By mandate,
the regulatory commissions are responsible for protecting the public interest. Does this mean, in our respondents view, that the commissions should take the

initiative in the formulation of policies affecting
the industries they regulate, or should the initiative be taken by the industries themselves with the
commissions serving a watchdog role? Or again, should
the initiative be left to the general public, working
through the mechanisms of the marketplace? Answers
were provided by the questionnaire.

A strong majority of respondents rejected the
suggestion that "initiative for business policies
which impinge directly on the public welfare" should
come from the regulators rather than the regulated
industries (Table 5.3(a)). Among the approximately
one-fifth that agreed with this suggestion, the only
apparent divergence was with respect to inertial
alignment. Predictably, those not aligned by inertia
appeared more inclined than any other subgroup to accept responsibility for initiating policy change.
Since the numbers involved were small (3 out of 7
agreeing with the suggestion), however, not much significance can be attached to this difference.

If in their opinion the regulators themselves
are not the proper agents for initiating policy in
protection of the public interest, in what manner
might industry be conceived as fulfilling that function? One possibility is that the policies industry
develops in pursuing its own self-interest might be
conceived as serving the public at large. Another is
that industry's interaction with the public under the
simulated free market conditions that regulation is
supposed to provide might be conceived as adequate in
itself for the public's protection. The first possibility was addressed by a questionnaire item suggesting that "the public is best served by the pursuit of
enlightened self-interest by private industry." In
their responses to this item the regulators showed no
consensus, but also showed no marked differences with
respect to alignment (Table 5.3(b)).

Conceptions of the role of the marketplace as
protector of the public interest were tested by another
series of questionnaire items. General reliance on
free market mechanisms was indicated by a virtually
unanimous agreement with the proposition that "the
consumer should be free to spend his income as he
chooses, with as little dictation from business or
government as possible" (Table 5.3(c)). At the same
time, very few respondents in any subgroup were willing

121

to agree that "the level of market demand for a good is the only feasible way of measuring the need for that good" (Table 5.3(d)). This combination of results suggests that, in the regulators' opinion, while public participation in the market should not be restrained by other interests, market demand should not be equated with consumer need. This latter is a significant finding in the context of electric power regulation, insofar as industry thinking accepts demand as a measure of need (Sayre, 1977, pp. 66, 280). Since ICC respondents were practically unanimous in their responses to both these items, however, again we must conclude that no significant differences appear with respect to alignment status.

One area in which a difference between aligned and nonaligned regulators clearly appeared was that of the relationship between regulation and the market process. As Tables 5.3(e) and (f) indicate, the inertially aligned were much more inclined as a group to subscribe to the traditional conception of regulation as simulating the effects of the free market, and much more sympathetic with the conception of the free market as itself protector of the public interest without regulation. This latter result is compatible with the defining characteristic of the inertially aligned, that they tend to avoid taking initiative on behalf of the public. Difference in this particular area, however, is not in itself sufficient to indicate any general pattern of difference between aligned and nonaligned regulators, since a small number of differences might be expected by chance.

Our findings thus are that no significant difference in conception exists between aligned and nonaligned regulators with respect to the composition of the public, with respect to policies that serve the public interest, or with respect to how such policies should be initiated. Since one's conception of these issues constitutes one's conception of the public interest as we have undertaken to measure it, our conclusion is that no significant difference in conception of the public interest exists between aligned and nonaligned regulators. The first part of the third hypothesis is thus disconfirmed.

Three interesting consequences follow from this result. The first concerns the academic literature

of regulatory "capture." This literature as a whole
is premised on the assumption the "capture" or alignment, however defined, constitutes an anomaly in the
regulator's attitude toward the public interest. Our
result suggests that even if a group of regulators
should turn out to be "captured" in one or another
manner, this condition does not necessarily make a
practical difference in their conception of the interest they are mandated to protect.

The second consequence is that our third hypothesis in its entirety must be set aside. Insofar as
there are no differences in conception of the public
interest between aligned and nonaligned regulators
within the ICC, our ethical analysis of Commission
values requires a new point of departure.

A new point of departure is indicated by the further consequence that the ICC's conception of the public interest may be treated as essentially homogeneous.
For purposes of ethical analysis we may leave questions
of alignment aside, and address the Commission as a
group with a uniform conception of the interest it is
mandated to serve.

NOTE

1. The nature of the items involved in this analysis precludes the use of difference-of-means tests as
in the previous comparisons. We have determined that
the only feasible mode of comparison for these simple
agree/disagree items is the use of percentages, even
though in so doing we violate a standard cannon of
statistical practice by computing percentages based
on small numbers of cases. Recognizing this difficulty, we must be highly conservative in interpreting
those differences which appear.

TABLE 5.1

Agreement with Selected Public Interest Items:
Who are the Public

Item

(a) Percent agreeing that "in contemporary society,
business managers must recognize responsibilities to many constituencies (e.g., employees,
customers, the public at large), not just to
their stockholders."

(b) Percent agreeing: "The ICC should make extensive attempts to eliminate social inequities by
assuming the role of principal advocate for low
income consumers as part of its regulatory function."

(c) Percent agreeing: "The obligations of businessmen and regulators alike are to current constituencies; they cannot reasonably be asked to
take the needs of future generations into account
in their decision-making."

TABLE 5.1 (continued)

Item	Decisional Aligned % (n)	Nonaligned % (n)	Associational Aligned % (n)	Nonaligned % (n)	Inertial Aligned % (n)	Nonaligned % (n)	ICC Total % (n)
(a)	100 (8)	90 (21)	100 (8)	94 (32)	94 (18)	100 (7)	95 (43)
(b)	0 (8)	14 (21)	12 (8)	12 (32)	11 (18)	14 (7)	12 (43)
(c)	0 (8)	0 (21)	0 (8)	9 (32)	0 (18)	0 (7)	7 (43)

125

TABLE 5.2

Agreement with Selected Public Interest Items:
What is in the Public Interest

Item

(a) Percent agreeing that "in the future we ought to define progress more in terms of an improved quality of life than in terms of growth in the GNP."

(b) Percent agreeing that "items such as air conditioning have become virtually indispensible to a moderate standard of living in this country."

(c) Percent agreeing: "The future well-being of our nation demands that we curtail the growth of our overall energy consumption."

(d) Percent agreeing that "the rate of growth in electrical consumption must slow down; we cannot continue doubling electrical consumption every decade."

(e) Percent favoring less growth in electric power use (slower growth, zero growth or negative growth).

(f) Percent favoring zero or negative growth in electric power use.

(g) Percent favoring present or more rapid rates of growth in electric power use.

(h) Percent agreeing that "the well-being of our society requires that we give less attention in the future to purely environmental matters than we have in the recent past."

(i) Percent approving a suggestion that the National Environmental Policy Act (NEPA) should be repealed.

TABLE 5.2 (continued)

Item

(j) Percent agreeing: "Nuclear power is currently the safest and most practical answer to our nation's energy needs."

(k) Percent including nuclear plants among the types of base load facilities they think ought to be built in Illinois in the foreseeable future.

(l) Percent agreeing that "the ICC should actively encourage the use of solar energy within its jurisdiction."

TABLE 5.2 (continued)

Item	Decisional Aligned % (n)	Nonaligned % (n)	Associational Aligned % (n)	Nonaligned % (n)	Inertial Aligned % (n)	Nonaligned % (n)	ICC Total % (n)
(a)	71 (7)	82 (27)	83 (6)	79 (38)	81 (16)	86 (7)	78 (40)
(b)	86 (7)	68 (28)	83 (6)	74 (38)	82 (17)	43 (7)	73 (41)
(c)	71 (7)	72 (21)	57 (7)	77 (31)	71 (17)	86 (7)	75 (40)
(d)	83 (6)	75 (20)	57 (7)	77 (31)	67 (15)	86 (7)	75 (40)
(e)	80 (5)	82 (17)	86 (7)	79 (24)	67 (15)	71 (7)	69 (39)
(f)	20 (5)	6 (17)	29 (7)	8 (24)	13 (15)	0 (7)	13 (39)
(g)	20 (5)	18 (17)	14 (7)	21 (24)	27 (15)	0 (7)	15 (39)
(h)	43 (8)	40 (20)	50 (6)	31 (32)	44 (16)	29 (7)	33 (40)
(i)	25 (4)	28 (18)	33 (3)	23 (26)	21 (14)	40 (5)	22 (32)
(j)	80 (5)	40 (20)	13 (8)	56 (27)	50 (16)	40 (5)	43 (37)
(k)	86 (7)	83 (18)	75 (8)	78 (27)	87 (15)	71 (7)	78 (37)
(l)	100 (8)	81 (21)	84 (8)	87 (31)	83 (18)	86 (7)	86 (42)

TABLE 5.3

Agreement with Selected Public Interest Items:
How to Achieve the Public Interest

Item

(a) Percent agreeing: "The initiative for changes in business policies which impinge directly on the public welfare should come from regulatory bodies; it is not the place of business to take the initiative in these matters."

(b) Percent agreeing: "The public is best served by the pursuit of enlightened self interest by private industry."

(c) Percent agreeing: "The consumer should be free to spend his income as he chooses, with as little dictation from business or government as possible."

(d) Percent agreeing that "the level of market demand for a good is the only feasible way of measuring the need for that good; if there is a high level of demand for electric power, we must assume that people need that much power."

(e) Percent agreeing: "Regulation should attempt to approximate the supply and price that would exist if energy were not provided by monopolies."

(f) Percent agreeing: "While regulation may be necessary in some specific instances, the market-place is the best protector of the general public interest in meeting our long term needs for abundant energy."

TABLE 5.3 (continued)

Item	Decisional Aligned %	(n)	Nonaligned %	(n)	Associational Aligned %	(n)	Nonaligned %	(n)	Inertial Aligned %	(n)	Nonaligned %	(n)	ICC Total %	(n)
(a)	12	(8)	24	(21)	0	(7)	25	(32)	11	(18)	43	(7)	19	(42)
(b)	71	(7)	65	(20)	43	(7)	68	(31)	76	(17)	50	(6)	64	(39)
(c)	100	(8)	95	(21)	86	(7)	97	(32)	94	(18)	100	(7)	93	(42)
(d)	25	(8)	15	(20)	14	(7)	16	(31)	28	(18)	0	(7)	17	(41)
(e)	50	(8)	67	(21)	86	(7)	61	(31)	50	(18)	86	(7)	63	(41)
(f)	62	(8)	48	(21)	38	(8)	50	(32)	61	(18)	29	(7)	49	(43)

130

6 Ethical Analysis of the ICC

FITTING PRACTICE TO THEORY

The method of analysis by which we propose to
examine the ICC's conception of the public interest
is what elsewhere we have called "ethical diagnosis"
(Sayre, 1977, Chapter 7). This method consists in
(1) detecting dominant patterns of priority and preference characterizing decisions of the agent in question; (2) correlating these patterns with conceptions
of obligation and of value that have been thoroughly
analyzed by moral theoreticians; and then with reference to these theoretical conceptions, (3) specifying
possible strengths and weaknesses of those decision-
patterns. Avoiding "subjective value judgments" in
favor of criticism representing effectively a consensus among scholars of moral theory, we thereby are
able to isolate aspects of the agent's normative thinking that warrant special notice in any evaluation of
its decision-making performance.

A basic assumption behind the method of ethical
diagnosis is that the individual person or organization
in question will follow certain preferences and prior-
itites in his or its routine decision-making. Although
in all likelihood the agent will not be aware of any
explicit ethical principles in its consideration of
options, these preferences and priorities may be viewed

131

as corresponding to principles of obligation and value of the sort traditionally dealt with by moral theory. In effect, we may view the decision-making performance of the agent as if that performance stemmed from a conscious application of explicit ethical principles, even though the agent may not even be acquainted with any ethical principles as such.

One possible means of correlating patterns of decision-making with ethical principles is to list all known principles of this sort individually, and to examine them seriatem for correlation with the agent's performance. Since principles of this sort are numerous if not indefinitely many, a more effective means of seeking correlations is to draw upon known characteristics of the agent's own conception of its obligations and preferences, and then to determine which of the many theoretical options fit this conception most closely. If more than one set of principles appear as possible candidates on this general basis, a more exact correspondence can be sought through a more detailed examination of empirical data.

A useful basis for correlation on a general theoretical level is provided by the characterization developed in the preceding chapter of the Commission's conception of the public interest it is obligated to serve. According to this characterization, pursuit of the public interest is conceived by the ICC generally as a matter of securing advantages for various constituencies--the advantages notably of electric power at reasonable rates for the public at large, including future as well as present persons, and of an adequate rate of return to investors to assure that the supply of power remains stable in a variable market. What makes certain policies or decisions (e.g., regarding rates or dividends) correct, that is to say, is the consequences that are expected to follow for the affected constituencies.

This emphasis upon consequences is indication that no adequate fit is likely to be found among ethical theories embodying conceptions of obligation to which consideration of consequences are either irrelevant or antithetical. One such account is that associated historically with Immanuel Kant, who maintained that what makes an act right or obligatory is the universalizability of the maxim by which the act is dic-

132

tated, irrespective of the consequences which in fact happened to follow. Another general type of account ruled out by a primary emphasis on consequences is the natural law theory, according to which an act is right or obligatory if it is prescribed by the nature of man and by man's place in the universe.

When we narrow the field from the outset to accounts of obligation stressing consequences, two classic theories emerge for further consideration. The better known of the two is probably utilitarianism, which dates back as an explicitly formulated ethical theory to the eighteenth Century, and whose nineteenth Century proponents (notably Bentham and J.S. Mill) used it as a theoretical basis for social and legal reform in England. In its simplist and most common formulation, utilitarianism is the theory that the right is what is best for the greatest number. To determine what is right, accordingly, is to determine the policy or course of action that maximizes good and minimizes evil for the greatest number of affected persons. This common formulation of utilitarianism is noteworthy for our purposes on several counts. First, it is a monistic account, in the sense that obligation in all cases of action or policy-formulation is grounded in a single basic principle--the so-called "principle of utility" dictating the greatest good for the greatest number. Second, it implies that moral decisions in principle can be based on an algorithm or routine calculational procedure. The "utiliarianism calculus" is a theoretical decision-procedure (strongly suggestive of contemporary cost-benefit analysis) in which advantages and disadvantages (goods and evils) for all persons involved are balanced against one another, with the most advantageous balance overall indicating what is right or morally obligatory. Third, utilitarianism thus formulated requires an independent conception of what constitutes the good or advantageous on the one hand, and the bad or disadvantageous on the other. In the case of Bentham, for example, the good was conceived as the pleasureful; but one might be utilitarian in theory of obligation without espousing hedonism as a theory of goodness. Finally, utilitarianism conceives of obligation as the greatest good for the greatest number aggregatively but not necessarily distributively. The right action or policy is one which leads to the greatest amount of good within the affected group

133

overall, not one which achieves the most even distribution of goods among persons within the group or the
best results for the group's least advantaged members.
Subject to more detailed examination, utilitarianism
in these respects provides at least an initially
plausible theoretical model for action in the public
interest which the ICC uniformly agrees is dictated
by their mandate.

The other classic theory suggested by this conception of the public interest may be called "deontological intuitionism," the former term indicating that
it is essentially a theory of duty (as distinct from
a theory pertaining essentially to value or goodness),
the second stressing moral sensitivity as a determinant of what is dutiful. This theory of obligation
also dates back to the eighteenth Century, particularly to the rationalism of that period (as represented, e.g., by Richard Price) and to the Moral Sense
School (represented, e.g., by Hutcheson). Characteristics of this theory relevant to our present purposes are the following. First, it is a pluralistic
account, meaning that it views moral decisions as
governed by a set of equally basic prima facie principles of conduct. Second, this theory denies the
possibility of any kind of algorithm or calculus for
moral decision-making, relying instead upon an assumption that moral agents possess a faculty of moral
insight or intuition by which to determine what is
dutiful in a given situation. Third, this theory may,
but also may not, require an independent account of
what is good for its application (whereas for utilitarianism such an account is always necessary). However, if one of the prima facie obligations recognized
by such a theory happens to prescribe pursuit of the
public interest, as has been the case with most versions of this theory defended in the current century
(e.g., by Pritchard, Ross and Frankena), then an account of what is good for the public is an essential
component. With an agency in view like the ICC, which
conceives itself responsible both to the public interest and to the interests of private investor-owned
utilities, some version of this theory stressing multiple responsibilities would also seem to be an antecedently plausible model.

The relevant theoretical differences between
these two models are illustrated by the following ex-

134

ample. Imagine a person who, when asked for a specification of his most general moral beliefs, mentioned
(1) the principle that one should avoid harming human
beings, and (2) the principle that one should speak
the truth. Knowing this much only about the person,
we would know relatively little about his normative
decision-making propensities. For one thing, he has
not disclosed what status he accords these principles
with respect to one another, particularly in situations where they come into conflict. One possible
way of specifying the content of these principles
would be, first, to define avoidance of harm as maximizing pleasure and minimizing displeasure and,
second, to interpret the principle prescribing truthfulness as derived from the principle prescribing
harm. A person completing the picture in this manner
as a utilitarian.

A deontological intuitionist, on the other hand,
would complete the account of his moral beliefs in a
rather more complex fashion. With respect to (1), he
might or might not consider it appropriate to provide
further specification of the notion of harming others.
Harm might be a matter of displeasure or absent benefit. Or it might be a characteristic he considers
recognizable by an active moral sense. Regardless of
the content of (1), however, he would treat both principles (1) and (2) as equally basic and equally encum-
bent upon his moral attention. Unlike the case with
the utilitarian, truthfulness would not be considered
obligatory only to the extent that it could be shown
to be a means for achieving good or avoiding harm.
Truthfulness would be taken as obligatory independently of its bearing upon the other principle. If
circumstances were to arise in which truthfulness and
harm to others seemed to be called for jointly, the
moral orientation of this person would lead him to
face both principles (1) and (2) as imposing prima
facie obligations and to rely upon his moral insight
to determine which should prevail. Both (1) and (2)
have status in their own right, and he must decide between them in much the same fashion as a referee in a
game might be called upon to adjudicate opposing claims
by two competitors which have equal prima facie validity. For convenience, let us refer to this account
of moral obligation as the "equal claim" account, in
contrast with the utilitarian account outlined in
previous paragraphs.

As this highly simplified example illustrates, to understand the configuration of an agent's moral beliefs we must for one thing know what principles of obligation he adheres to. This will tell us the values he considers himself duty-bound to strive for in action. But we must also know how he interprets those values--what in fact counts as harming other people, or what goods are to be maximized for the greatest number. That is to say, we must know the theory of value he espouses (or behaves as if he espouses) as well as his theory of obligation. Finally, we must know how the moral principles he adheres to are interrelated. Are they all derivative from a single principle of obligation, as with classic utilitarianism, or do they include more than one underived principle with prima facie standing, as is typical of what we are calling the "equal claim" model? Data acquired through answers to questionnaire items enabled us to specify these variables for the ICC.

The mandate of the Commission requires its members and its employees to conduct their business so as to insure the public at large access to electric power at nonexploitive prices, and so as to assure acceptable rates of return for the private investors who provide that service. To avoid ambiguity regarding this mandate, we asked all respondents to agree with or to correct the following statement of the general theory behind regulation.

"Regulation of certain industries is necessary because these industries tend toward monopoly, insofar as the firms in these industries operate most efficiently under monopolistic conditions. In the absence of the free market mechanisms which handle the problems of allocation and pricing, regulation exists to insure to the public non-discriminatory access to service at reasonable cost, while also securing reasonable rates of return to the providers of service."

All but a very few respondents endorsed this statement explicitly, and those who chose to make corrections were concerned more with the rationale than with the content of the mandate. Without qualification, we may conclude that the respondents agree that their mandate as regulators includes two principles of obliga-

136

tion: (A) that they work to insure the public non-discriminatory access to power at reasonable rates, and (B) that they work to assure reasonable rates of return on investment.

Knowing this much about the obligations recognized by members of the ICC, however, is not enough to determine which ethical theory (if either) characterizes their normative decision-making. For acceptance of those two principles of obligation is compatible with both the utilitarian and the "equal claim" models. Differences with respect to these models begin to appear only when we consider possible relationships of dependency between the principles. If the decision-making patterns of a regulator espousing principles (A) and (B) above are best modeled by utilitarian theory, then this individual will (when pressed, or when reflective about the matter) tend to view both (A) and (B) as derivative from a more basic principle prescribing the greatest good for the greatest number of affected persons. Such a regulator, for example, might upon reflection agree that his most basic duty is to assure the well-being of the public within his jurisdiction, and explain that reasonable costs of power and reasonable rates of return on investment are means of achieving well-being for the persons affected. The question then would arise what that regulator conceives well-being to amount to (e.g., health, happiness, freedom of choice, economic solvency), and how he conceives the public to which he is obligated (e.g., rate-payers in his service area exclusively, all citizens young and old, the human race generally). Knowing these things, we would have a good picture of the general structure at least of his acknowledged duty.

If the normative decision-making of a person accepting (A) and (B) were best modeled by the "equal claim" theory, on the other hand, then he would tend upon reflection to think of these principles as binding independently of any more basic obligation. When faced with a conflict in application between the two principles (for example, a case similar to the recent "Three Mile Island" incident in which financial penalties to either investor or consumer seem inevitable), then he would view his role as one calling for judgment between the two interests on the basis of informed sensitivity unaided by algorithmic decision-procedures.

137

Thus far in this Chapter we have seen (1) that our respondents' conception of the interests they are obligated to serve lays stress upon the consequences of their official decisions, (2) that this stress upon consequences strongly suggests either utilitarianism or the "equal claim" account (or both) as theoretical counterpart of their decision-making patterns, and (3) that utilitarianism and the "equal claim" account thus applied differ primarily in their conception of the relationship between utility interests and the public interest generally. According to the utilitarian model, interests of utility managers and stockholders have standing only as derivative from a general principle prescribing the greatest good for the greatest number of affected persons. Insofar as the public is well served by a regulated industry, and insofar as the solvency of that industry requires (among other things) a given rate of return on investment, the regulator has an obligation to allow that rate of return. But the regulator is under no obligation to protect the interests of the utility apart from its contribution to the general good. According to the "equal claim" model, on the other hand, both utility and public interests have standing in their own right, and the regulator's duty in his decision-making is to weigh the claims of these two factions as an independent judge or referee, without benefit of priorities provided by a general principle of obligation.

This distinction between the utilitarian and the "equal claim" models may remind the reader of a distinction drawn in Chapter One between two historically important conceptions of the regulatory process. The conception generally accompanying the Conventional Theory of Regulation is that the regulatory process is for the protection of the public. In the absence of free market forces, the regulatory commission is charged with responsibility for assuring the public reliable service at fair rates from a monopolistic enterprise. A competing conception stresses the constitutional right of a business enterprise to receive just compensation for any appropriation of its property, which converts into a right of the industry to receive a just return on investment. According to this second conception, which has been active for at least the better part of the present century, the duty of the regulators is to act as neutral arbitrator between the claims of industry and the claims of the public.

138

A prominent advocate of this second conception was Samuel Insull, who complained in 1924 (see p. 13 above) that many "newly created" commissions thought that their function is to represent the public and not merely to judge between public and utility.

Although neither Insull nor early representatives of the Conventional Theory conceived the issue in terms of moral theory, the difference between them corresponds precisely to the difference between the utilitarian and the "equal claim" models of regulatory duty. Like the Conventional Theory of Regulation, the utilitarian account of obligation conceives the regulator as responsible primarily to the public interest, subordinating the private interests of industry to this broader concern. Like the view espoused by Insull, on the other hand, the "equal claim" account conceives both industry and public as having rights which the regulator should recognize in his role of neutral arbitrator. When conflict arises between these individual interests, the regulator must judge on a case-by-case basis.

This parallel between views of regulation and theories of obligation has dual significance for our analysis. For one thing, it strongly corroborates our choice of the utilitarian and the "equal claim" accounts as the most promising models of regulatory decision-making. In fact, it suggests that patterns of decision fitting both models will be found within our sample. Equally important, however, is the indication it affords that the critical results of our ethical diagnosis will respond to issues posed by the regulatory process in a practical setting. If relevant strengths and weaknesses of the two ethical models appear to differ significantly, then this should reflect upon the adequacy of the two competing views of regulation.

CLASSIFICATION AND RESULTS

Regulators were grouped under the utilitarian and the "equal claim" models according to their responses to certain items on the questionnaire. Normative decision-making following the utilitarian model is explicitly indicated, first, by an affirmative ("agree" or "strongly agree") response to the following

questionnaire item: "A good decision is one which
results in the most benefit for the greatest number
of persons." Emphasis upon benefits to society at
large, as well as subordination of the economic well-
being of the utility to the benefit of society as a
whole, is explicitly indicated, secondly, by an affirmative response to the questionnaire item: "The
regulation of utilities should reflect the philosophy that regulation is necessary because society as
a whole benefits from an insured supply of energy and
would be harmed by an economic decision to withhold
supply." Third, inclusion of utility interest within
a wider public interest is indicated by an affirmative
response to the questionnaire item suggesting that
"the public is best served by the pursuit of enlightened self-interest by private industry." Finally,
de-emphasis of utility in favor of public interest is
indicated by failure to mention the former while
featuring the latter in response to an invitation on
the questionnaire to state what the respondent considered to be the central responsibility of the ICC.
None of these four indicators, of course, is wholly
unambiguous. A person might agree with the third
item, for instance, as a rationale for economic self-
determination by industry, with no intent of de-empha-
sizing the importance of this factor. In view of possible ambiguities, positive responses to three of
these four indicators was accepted as our criterion of
utilitarian thinking.

Normative decision-making of the sort modeled by
the "equal claim" theory is indicated, first, by a
pointed rejection of the basic principle that a good
decision is one resulting in the greatest good for the
greatest number--that is, by a negative response ("disagree" or "strongly disagree") to the first questionnaire item mentioned above. Equal status of public
and utility interests is indicated, second, by an equal
emphasis on the two in the respondent's description of
the central responsibility of the ICC (the fourth item
above). Equal status of these two sets of interests
is also indicated, thirdly, by a top ranking in importance given to the option "what the majority of both
public interest groups and public utilities would find
acceptable" in response to the question "What, in your
judgment, is the ultimate criterion generally operative
in the ICC decision-making for deciding what is or is
not in the public interest?", in conjunction with an

140

affirmative answer to the question "Is this the criterion you personally believe should be used?" Finally, the availability of any algorithmic decision-
procedure is explicitly denied by selection of the
option "what the ICC commissioners finally and reflectively prefer" in response to the previous question, along with an indication of agreement with that
criterion. Consideration of ambiguity similar to
those mentioned above led us to accept positive indications on three of these four items as our criterion
for thinking according to the "equal claim" model.

Application of these criteria produced the following results. Of the 39 regulators responding to
relevant parts of the questionnaire, 31 exhibited
preference patterns typical of utilitarian normative
thinking, 7 exhibited preference patterns typical of
"equal claim" thinking, and 2 exhibited neither pattern. The fact that one respondent met criteria for
both types of normative thinking suggests either that
our criteria are not infallible (which is likely),
that this respondent is not consistent in his normative thinking (which is possible), or both (which also is possible). In any case, decision-making in the
ICC clearly is dominated by normative thinking of a
utilitarian character, with a distinct trace also of
the "equal claim" mentality.

NORMATIVE CONSEQUENCES

Both utilitarianism and deontological intuitionism (what we have called the "equal claim" account)
are classic theories of obligation, with strengths
and weaknesses that have been thoroughly examined by
moral theoreticians. To the extent that these theories provide apt models of normative thinking within
the ICC, we should expect to find indications of both
these strengths and weaknesses in that group's decision-making.

A clear strength represented by both utilitarianism and the "equal claim" theory is the element of
explicit social concern. A moral agent guided by
utilitarian principles would consider it his duty to
avoid action that would bring advantage to isolated
groups at the expense of the wider community, and
would instead stress action that works for the bet-

141

terment of society generally. A similar stress on
the general welfare is present in deontological intuitionism, the main difference being that the latter
theory might give equal weight to more isolated interests.

Indications of major concern for the public at
large are found in responses to five of the eight
hypothetical scenarios presented. for the regulator's
consideration. One scenario posed the alternative
between constructing a coal-burning power plant within
the confines of a community with a high incidence of
lung disease and bringing power from a distance over
difficult terrain. Respondents were asked to agree
or to disagree with the decision made by the power
company concerned, and then to explain the reasons
for their attitude. These responses were independently coded[1] as indicating primary concern either
for the community or for the power company. Of the
26 responses interpretable in this regard, 17 (65
percent) indicated primary concern for the community.
Another hypothetical situation involved construction
of an energy-intensive plant in a predominantly rural
area, with results that would probably benefit the
power company considerably more than the community at
large. Coding of responses to this situation revealed
16 out of 20 unambiguous opinions in favor of the community, or 80 percent of the total. Results similar-
ly derived from the remaining three scenarios showed
percentages to the same effect of 62 percent, 80 percent and 60 percent respectively. In each case, a
clear majority of respondents who expressed opinions
on such matters at all explicitly favored community
against exclusive private interests.

Along with this stress upon the general welfare
goes a weakness of utilitarian thinking that has long
been recognized as one of its major drawbacks--its
emphasis upon collective as against distributive
goods. In an extreme situation, the utilitarian principle might even prescribe harming a minority to bring
advantage to the majority. If it were the case, for
example, that 75 percent of a population (say its
wealthy and moderately well-to-do members) could be
benefited by economic policies that would harm the
remaining 25 percent, and even if the harm to the
minority were twice as extensive as the benefit to the
majority, then (other things being equal) those poli-

cies would be prescribed by utilitarian thinking.

This particular weakness is not inherent in deontological intuitionism, inasmuch as the rights of
any given minority might figure among the interests
to which the moral agent feels he has independent
prima facie obligation. However, in our application
of the "equal claimant" model in which only one set
of rights is recognized beyond those of the public
at large--i.e., the rights of the regulated industry--
shortcomings of this same character are likely to be
present. Insofar as any minority other than industry
is represented only as part of the general public,
the interests of that minority may be submerged to
its disadvantage within the interests of the public
conceived collectively. A consequence is that thinking characterized by this model, as well as by utilitarianism, is likely to exhibit shortcomings with respect to distribution of benefits.

Indications of a tendency to favor collective
over distributive benefits were provided both by the
hypothetical scenarios and by the questionnaire. One
hypothetical situation posed to the respondents por-
trayed a dilemma between flooding a farm area to ac-
quire additional hydroelectric generating capacity,
and preserving the interests of an ethnic minority
inhabiting the land concerned. Of 21 responses that
could confidently be coded, 13 (62 percent) stressed
the interests of the community at large and the remainder (38 percent) stressed those of the minority
group.[2] A more forceful indication that distributive
benefits do not figure prominently in ICC thinking
appeared in responses to a questionnaire item suggesting the "The ICC should make extensive attempts
to eliminate social inequities by assuming the role
of principal advocate for low income consumers as part
of its regulatory function." A resounding 38 of 42
respondents (90 percent) rejected this suggestion.[3]

The upshot, we hasten to add, is not necessarily
that the ICC is remiss in not giving more weight to
considerations of distribution in its thinking about
public benefits. It is rather that, true to predic-
tions based upon our two normative models, when regulators in the ICC are posed with decision-situations
in which distributive are pitted against collective
benefits they tend rather strongly to favor the lat-

ter. While it is not the case that this tendency always results in bad normative decisions, it does constitute a potential weakness of Commission thinking that the agency might want to examine carefully for purposes of self-understanding.

One further shortcoming of utilitarian thinking which has been well explored by moral theoreticians is a tendency to limit the range of persons to which a moral agent considers himself responsible in applying the principle of the greatest good to the greatest number. Paradoxical as it may seem, this tendency is a natural outgrowth of essential features of the utilitarian principle itself. Emphasis upon the greatest good in the first place carries with it a commitment in principle to approach goods as numerically comparable quantities, just as emphasis upon the greatest number of beneficiaries overall requires enumerating the group of affected persons. Since no attempt to calculate total amounts of goods and evils can be undertaken if the number of persons affected is not finite, any attempt to think of the "human race in general" (or some comparably indefinite body of persons) is impractical from the outset. The result is that utilitarians who make a serious effort to apply their principles in practice are constrained to limit their concern to a geographically or socially restricted group of beneficiaries, such as Europeans, Americans, or even citizens of Illinois. For similar reasons, the same type of restriction must occur with respect to time.

Although this weakness is not intrinsic to deontological intuitionism as such, again it goes with the "equal claim" model in this application. That is, since one obligation recognized within the strain of "equal claim" thinking found within the ICC is an obligation to society at large, the same difficulty will appear as that of the utilitarian in delimiting the range of persons concerned. In the context of either mode of thinking, geographical and spatial limitations will pose a problem.

Obvious geographical restrictions in the thinking of our group of respondents are implied in the theory of regulation, as stated in the text above. A large majority agreed with this theory as a statement of their responsibility to the "public." The content of

144

this responsibility, however, is that they should insure "nondiscriminatory access to service at reasonable cost." And the only persons to whom they are
thus responsible are the rate-payers of the state of
Illinois. In effect, the "public" to which they are
responsible is severely limited in a geographic sense.
The presence of temporal limitations upon this "public," in turn, is indicated by their responses previously cited to the question "How long a time span
would you be thinking of if you were to use the expression 'long-run' in the context of your work?",
to which the median response was about ten years.
Given this limitation--despite their strong rejection
of the suggestion that future generations should not
figure in their decision-making (cited above)--it appears that for practical purposes they consider concern for more than the present generation beyond their
competency.

A basic shortcoming of the "equal claim" model
to which utilitarian thinking is not subject is its
systematic lack of any principle for arbitrating competing claims of the different constituencies it rec-
ognizes. Whereas normative thinking after the utilitarian model subordinates all claims to the general
principle of the greatest good for the greatest number, thinking after the "equal claim" model accepts
no general guidelines for arbitration in cases of
conflict. The agent given to this mode of thinking
has nothing to rely on beyond his "sense of duty."
And since an individual's "sense of duty" may well
seem arbitrary to other persons, this mode of thinking is hard to defend against charges of capricious-
ness.

The presence of this weakness in the "equal
claim" strain of ICC decision-making is reflected in
the third indication of that mode of thinking ex-
plained in the preceding section--identification of
"what the ICC commissioners finally and reflectively
prefer" as the criterion generally used within the
ICC for deciding what is or is not in the public interest.

Whereas normative decision-making after the
utilitarian and the "equal claim" models is on a par
with respect to the strengths and weaknesses previously examined, in this final respect the latter is more

distinctly deficient. It would appear, as a consequence, that the associated conception of regulation
as a matter of neutral arbitration should not predom-
inate as an ideal for the individual regulator to
follow.

The most noteworthy results of this analysis are
(1) that normative thinking in the ICC is characteristically (a) strong in its emphasis upon the social
good, (b) weak in its consideration for collective
over distributive benefits, and (c) weak in its tendency to limit its concern to fewer persons than are
affected by its decision-making; and (2) that this
thinking exhibits distinct conceptions of obligation
that might come into conflict in times of crisis. A
possible illustration of this latter is provided by
the recent Three Mile Island incident, to which (as
noted above) utilitarian and "equal claimant" thinking might well have different responses.

These indications of possible strengths and weaknesses in ICC normative thinking are not offered by
way of negative moral criticism. They are offered as
features upon which the Commission might focus in an
effort to evaluate its own decision-making.

NOTES

1. Three persons associated with the construction of the instrument interpreted the results independently in view of the attitudes it was intended to
test. Agreement in interpretation by at least two of
the three coders was required for a given response to
count as data.

2. A ratio of scarcely more than three to two
against the minority is not a conclusive indication
of a general rejection of minority rights within the
Commission. This result is all the more ambiguous because various extraneous factors (e.g., the respondent once lived on a farm, or is a strong supporter
of hydroelectric power) could have influenced a choice
for or against the ethnic group. At best we can say
that the data show a majority of our respondents declining to choose in favor of minority rights.

3. Again we must avoid laying too much stress

upon this result. Since Illinois law is understood
by at least some of our respondents to prohibit special rate consideration for low income customers,
these respondents may simply have subordinated their
sense of what ought to be to their realization of what
is in fact the case.

REFERENCE

Sayre, K.M. (ed.) (1977), Values in the Electric Power
Industry, University of Notre Dame Press, Notre
Dame, Indiana.

7 Conclusions

A FURTHER LOOK AT THE ACADEMIC THEORIES

If the hypotheses posed for empirical testing in Chapter Two had all been confirmed, the consequences for the theoretical literature regarding regulatory "capture" would have relatively straightforward. Taking the ICC as a paradigm commission for a detailed case study, our first hypothesis was that we would find a significant number of regulators (commissioners and staff) among this group who were not aligned with ("captured" by) the industry they are entrusted to regulate. Under the provisional assumption that a significant number of nonaligned regulators would be found, we hypothesized next that aligned and nonaligned regulators would exhibit different profiles on standard value tests. The purpose of this second hypothesis was to explore the general conjecture that the academic theories of regulation, in overlooking the values brought to their task by individual regulators, are leaving out of account a factor that has an important bearing on the outcome of the regulatory process. In an attempt to devise a technique by which the value orientations of individual regulators could be objectively appraised, finally, we posed the further hypothesis that the differences in value structures between aligned and nonaligned regulators could be correlated with differences between standard theories of normative judgment,

148

the strengths and weaknesses of which are antecedently well known.

If all three hypotheses had been confirmed, the consequence with respect to the academic theories would have been that "capture" cannot be predicted solely on the basis of the factors (association, dependency, diversion, etc.) with which these theories have been preoccupied. To anticipate the extent to which a given regulator would be subject to "capture," we would have to know something about his value orientation as well.

While the first hypothesis was confirmed, however, the second was partially disconfirmed, and the third rendered pointless as initially construed. Even so, this study has not left the academic theories unscathed. Our most interesting results with regard to these theories arose from attempts to operationalize the notions of "capture" upon which they are predicated. To operationalize these notions is to specify forms of thinking or behavior which could be accepted as indications of the various types of "capture" in question. As the study proceeded, however, it became increasingly clear that the academic literature as a body not only muddles the several types of "capture" together but also lacks precision regarding forms of behavior to which this term applies as a descriptive category. At the same time, the term 'capture' has more than a merely descriptive force, since the academic theories almost invariably generate strong normative conclusions about the dire consequences of "capture"--conclusions frequently reached without firm empirical evidence.

To strip this language of some of its emotive force, we replaced the term 'capture' by the more neutral term 'alignment'. We then distinguished eight apparently different types of alignment discussed in the literature, and singled out five which we could measure in the decision-making behavior of our individual respondents. These five types of alignment were operationalized in terms of specific responses to two questionnaires, one engaging the regulator in hypothetical situations calling for normative decision-making and the other evoking judgments about the proper conduct of regulation. It was through data obtained by these measures that our three hypothesis were put to

149

test.

Two findings of particular interest emerged from
our efforts to examine these notions of alignment in
operationally specific form. One concerns dependency
relationships among the several types of alignment.
A high positive correlation appeared between cliental
and decisional alignment, indicating that individuals
who emphasize utility interests in discussing the rationale of the regulatory process are also likely to
issue decisions favoring the utilities they regulate.
Equally intelligible is the high positive correlation
we found between associational and dependency alignment, indicating that regulators strongly dependent
upon the utilities for needed information are likely
to come into contact frequently with utility representatives. More surprising was the negative correlation between dependency and decisional alignment,
meaning that individuals reliant upon the utilities
for information seem distinctly disinclined to favor
the utilities in their decision-making. Apart from
these three statistically significant correlations,
the types of alignment for which we tested appeared
independent.

Our second finding of interest in this regard
is a basic distinction between what we came to call
"structural" (or "indirect") and "personal" alignment. A majority of regulators who turned out to be
aligned in any sense at all were aligned only in that
they view the regulatory process as essentially reactive, calling for little initiative on their part in
behalf of the public interest. Indeed, approximately
three-fourths of our respondents shared this view of
their function, which we labeled 'inertial alignment'.
Inertial and dependency alignment have been grouped
under the heading of "structural" or indirect alignment because they result from the very structure of
the regulatory task, either in itself or in the view
of the individuals concerned, and because they do not
directly affect decisions. A much smaller percentage
were aligned in a sense involving personal commitment
to utility interests, ("personal" alignment) as exem-
plified by decisional (27 percent) and cliental (zero
percent) alignment. Since it is alignment in these
senses only that converts into direct action on the
utilities' behalf (hence the label "direct" alignment), our conclusion with respect to the first hy-

pothesis was that only 27 percent of the regulators
in the ICC sample are aligned in any sense constituting a possible impediment to the proper functioning of the regulatory process.

It must be noted that the structural or indirect
types of alignment do not in themselves prevent the
regulators from acting consistently in the public
interest. At worst, they delimit the scope of actions
the regulators might take in representing that interest. The limitations inherent in these indirect types
of alignment ought not be judged automatically as un-
desirable or sinister, as academic theory in its normative passion has tended to judge them. On the contrary, it might be argued that a reactive tendency on
the part of the regulatory commission reflects its
proper role within our political system, where fundamental policy changes are expected to be initiated by
the highly visible and accessible legislative process.

Our conclusion with respect to the second hypothesis was that there is no difference in general pattern of value orientation between aligned and nonaligned regulators in the ICC, for any of the five
types of alignment tested. However, several statistically significant differences in particular value
rankings appeared between the decisionally aligned and
nonaligned, which added up to what appears to be an
emphasis among the decisionally aligned on the "old-
fashioned" conservative values of individualism and
patriotism.

The fact that alignment in the ICC is not correlated with differences in general value orientation
does not vindicate the academic theories in remaining
silent on the role of individual values in the regulatory process. Since decisional alignment is the
type most likely to have direct practical effects,
the appearance of a strong correlation between this
type of alignment and a distinctive set of individual
values suggests, to the contrary, that personal values
may be a factor influencing the outcome of the regulatory process.

Our general finding with respect to the third hypothesis is that there is no difference between aligned
and nonaligned regulators with respect to their conception of the public interest they are mandated to

serve. However, a difference did appear between the conception of the public interest shared by most of our respondents in the ICC and the conception shared by most utility executives (see Sayre, 1977). Since appropriation of the utilities' conception of what is in the public interest would be expected to be part of the phenomenon of "capture" as treated by the academic literature, and since the ICC is one of the oldest regulatory agencies in the country, this finding counts as evidence against one of the most basic tenets of the academic theories—that all regulatory agencies tend eventually to be "captured" by the industries they regulate. A summary of our findings comparing the regulators' with the utilities' conception of the public interest is presented in the following section, with further observations about the academic theories.

COMPARISON BETWEEN ICC AND UTILITY RESPONDENTS

While cross-sample comparisons are inherently interesting, it is of particular interest to examine the value profiles of the ICC regulators in comparison with those of typical industry representatives. Similarity of values may augur similarity in judgments regarding the public good, while differences in values may lead to misunderstanding and conflict. This section compares values of the ICC with those of the utilities, insofar as we have data (from Sayre, 1977) on comparable items.

Of the three standarized values tests administered to the ICC, two were also completed by the utility executives: the Allport Study of Values, and the California Life Goals Evaluation Schedules (CLGES). On the Allport test, the utility executives scored significantly higher than the norm (the population at large) on the theoretical and the economic interest scales, and significantly lower on the social and aesthetic scales. As indicated in Chapter Four, the ICC respondents generally resembled the population at large, except for lower scores on the social (see footnote 5, Chapter 5, p. 93) and religious dimensions.

A comparison of ICC and utility samples (Table 7.1) shows that the former are both less theoretical and less oriented toward economic matters than the

latter. This result could be reasonably anticipated,
inasmuch as more than half of the utility respondents
are either engineers (who typically score high on the
theoretical scale) or businessmen (who typically score
high on the economic dimension). Nor is it surprising
to note that the ICC respondents showed more interest
in the political realm, since their role is created
in response to political pressures. A practical consequence of these differences is that we would expect
utility representatives to stress economic and theoretical aspects of a case at issue (a proposed rate increase, for example), while the regulators might be
more concerned with its political aspects. Insofar
as the regulators resemble the general public more
closely in values than do the executives, however,
we would expect the decisions of the former more often to reflect the will of the public.

The other standardized test on which we have data
for both groups is the CLGES. As Chapter Four indicates, the regulators are motivated more than is the
public generally by life goals of leadership and self-
expression, and less motivated by esteem and social
service. The utility executives, on the other hand,
registered statistically significant differences from
the general public on eight of the ten dimensions of
this test (Table 7.2). Like our ICC respondents, they
scored much lower than the public on the esteem and
social service scales. But they were much higher than
the public on the scales measuring the goals of profit, fame and leadership. They are less concerned
than the public with independence and security, and
more motivated by the goal of interesting experiences.

A comparison of ICC and utility scores, nonetheless, shows less difference than exists between either
set and the scores constituting the norm.[1] On most
dimensions, in fact, the ICC respondents stand some-
where between the utility executives and the general
public, an interesting position symbolically when one
thinks of the regulator as a mediator between the
utilities and the public they serve. ICC scores on
the CLGES differ notably from those of the company
executives in our earlier study only in displaying
significantly less orientation toward profit. This is
not unexpected, inasmuch as the literature on regulation consistently stresses that being a regulator is
relatively unrewarding financially. The main interest

of this finding is with respect to the "self-interest" theory of regulatory "capture" (see Chapter One), which maintains that individual desire for profit inevitably will lead the regulator to align himself with the regulated industry in hopes of future reward. Since that theory predicts capture on self-serving economic grounds for the commissioners specifically, it is particularly noteworthy that the scores on the profit dimension for the five present or past commissioners in our sample were without exception lower even than the mean score of the ICC as a group. Since profit does not appear to be a particularly strong personal life goal for this group of respondents at least, we find yet another reason to be dissatisfied with any theory of "capture" based on self-interest of the regulator.

Questionnaires administered to the two groups of respondents differed considerably in characteristics they were designed to test. Aspects in which comparison of results nonetheless is relevant and plausible are conveniently grouped under the three headings explored in Chapter Five pertaining to the public interest. Our approach to the topic in that context, it may be recalled, was to characterize the regulators' conception of the public interest in terms of their response to the following three questions: (1) who belongs to the public the interests of which are being considered? (2) what policies best serve the interests of this public?; and (3) by what means are these policies best initiated and implemented? Although questions such as these did not figure in the construction of the questionnaires administered to the utility executives, plausible answers in their behalf can be constructed from other data and compared with summaries of how the regulators responded.

As Table 5.1(a) illustrates, almost all regulators in our group consider utility management responsible to a variety of constituencies, including employees and stockholders as well as consumers. At the same time, virtually all regulators consider it their business to oversee the manner in which industry serves these various groups. Since the same constituencies were emphasized as figuring in their mandate by executives from both utilities sampled in the previous study (Sayre, 1977, pp. 190-191), there appears to be no essential difference between executives and regulators regarding who constitutes the public to which they are responsible respectively. Equally unambiguous is the agreement between executives and regulators on the issue whether rate structure should be used to help resolve social inequities, with over four-fifths of both groups (Table 5.1(b) above; Sayre, 1977, p. 279) rejecting this use as inappropriate. Comparisions with regard to perceived obligations to future generations, on the other hand, are not so straightforward. Whereas most regulators, when asked, agreed that interests of future generations should figure in their decision-making, (Table 5.1 (c)) no utility executives mentioned concerns of this sort when discussing issues stemming from use of various power sources (nuclear in particular; Sayre, 1977, p. 277). On the other hand, the term 'long range' in the expression "long range planning" meant something in the order of 30 years for the executives (ibid.) and only about 10 years for the regulators. In effect, the executives seem to think in terms more compatible with concern for future generations than do the regulators, although such concern is more explicitly part of the thinking of the latter group.

By contrast, rather sharp differences appear between the executives and the regulators in their responses indicative of what policies they conceive best to serve the public interest. On the topic of rates of increase in energy consumption, for a notable example, approximately 75 percent of the regulators believe that deceleration of such rates are in the public interest (Table 5.2(c)), while less than one-third of our (NIPSCO) executives expressed that opinion (Sayre, 1977, p. 164). On another significant point of comparison, while approximately 50 percent of the regulators consider nuclear power to be the safest and most promising answer to our country's energy needs (Table 5.2(j)), over 90 percent of the executives expressed that view of the nuclear option (Sayre, 1977, p. 164). Since rapidly increasing energy consumption and nuclear power are among the most controversial energy issues facing our country today, the fact that regulatory thinking on these topics sharply differs from utility thinking in our samples is a further indication that respondents in the ICC are not "captured" by the industry they regulate.

155

Further differences worthy of note appear in a comparison of utility and regulatory thinking with regard to how policies in the public interest ought to be initiated and implemented. The academic literature on regulation is shot through with references to the role of regulation by commission as an impartial means of keeping industry in line, in effect relieving industry itself of the need to exercise much concern over the social impact of its operations (Chapter One above). The same attitude toward regulation as a source of normative control appeared with the data of the previous study (Sayre, 1977, pp. 194 and 282 in particular). In a word, utility executives tend generally to be content with a division of responsibility in which they are accountable for the reliability of their service and the regulators are accountable for its impact upon society at large. Sharp exception to this attitude on the part of the ICC is evident in Table 5.3(a), which shows a proportion not exceeding 20 percent in favor of a statement relieving industry from responsibility for the public impact of its policies. This finding is one of the most cautionary to stem from our pair of studies, with neither industry nor regulation accepting primary responsibility for setting policy in the public interest. The middle ground on the matter may well be the most reasonable, with industry and regulation alike sharing part of the responsibility. This middle ground, of course, is compatible with the attitude of the ICC found in our data. But if a particular utility should be unwilling to take its part of the responsibility seriously, more of the burden is placed upon the regulators than they are ready to bear. One of the most urgent needs for reform indicated by this pair of studies may well be the need for a clear location of primary responsibility to the public in matters of policy initiation and implementation.

A significant point of consensus with respect to policy is seen in the overwhelming agreement of the regulators (implied by data in Table 5.3(c)) with a statement affirming that the consumer should be free to buy power for whatever purpose he chooses. This correlates with an emphatic endorsement of the same freedom appearing time and again in our conversations with power company executives during the previous study. On the other hand, an equally significant point of disagreement comes with the regulators' conception of the relationship between power needs and power wants. Whereas a utility's case for increased generating capacity typically is based upon an equation of what society wants (what it will pay for) with what it needs by way of electric power (Sayre, 1977, pp. 279-280), approximately 80 percent of the regulators rejected this equation (Table 5.3(d). If our previous analysis of this assumption of identity between needs and wants as not being in the public interest is accurate (Sayre, 1977, pp. 83-86), and if the regulatory commission is the only officially constituted body that is inclined to question this assumption, then the question arises why regulatory commissions ought not be given an active role in the evaluation of environmental impact statements required for new plant construction. This is the context in which this assumption has its most notable impact.

The most obvious point of comparison between utility and regulatory normative decision-making comes with the the results of ethical modeling. Our present finding in this regard is that normative decision-making among the regulators follows a pattern appropriately modeled by utilitarian theory, with a minor strain of "equal claim" thinking. Apparently similar results were obtained by an application of the same technique to utility decision-making in the previous study, where utilitarian thinking was blended with an equally dominant strain of ethical egoism (maximization of self-interest as the primary principle of responsibility). At first glance, the appearance of utilitarianism as a major component of the normative model characterizing both groups suggests an alignment of some basic sort, albeit perhaps one not recognized in the academic literature.

This initial appearance of alignment, however, is illusory for a reason that must be deemed decisive. The combination of utilitarian and egoistic thinking on the part of utility management means that normative decisions in that domain are directed toward the achievement of maximized benefits, and that the benefits concerned are in behalf of the utilities and the public alike. In the egoistic-utilitarian mode of thinking, both constituencies have standing in their own right, neither being subordinated to the other's interests. But it is precisely this independent status of both utility and public interest that is re-

157

jected by the utilitarianism characteristic of our group of regulators. The model according equal status to these two interests in the thinking of the ICC, it may be recalled, is what we have been refering to as the "equal claim" model, which stands in opposition to the utilitarianism of the regulators which accords independent status to the interests of no special interest group. Contrary to initial appearance, the utilitarianism of the regulators does not constitute agreement with the utilities in this regard.

TOPICS FOR SELF-ASSESSMENT WITHIN THE COMMISSION

Two classic weaknesses of utilitarian thinking for which evidence was found among ICC respondents are (1) that it tends to ignore considerations of equity (i.e., it stresses collective over distributive benefits), and (2) that it tends in application to restrict unduly the range of persons whose benefits are considered. To say that these are weaknesses of utilitarian thinking is not to say, however, that ignoring considerations of equity and restricting the range of concerned persons are necessarily morally wrong in all practical contexts. In the case of the ICC in particular, it must be recognized that one very influential reason why some respondents rejected the option of providing special rates for low income persons (an indication of deemphasis on distributive benefits discussed in Chapter Six) is that they construe Illinois law as expressly prohibiting such rates. Since regulation in Illinois proceeds within the laws of that state, the weakness (if a weakness is involved at all) must be attributed to the Legislature instead of the Commission. Similar restraints would appear to dictate that the Commission be primarily concerned with the interests of persons presently living within the state.

The finding that ICC decision-making fails to exhibit concern for equity, and for the interest of all persons affected by its decisions, thus is no grounds in itself for passing moral judgment. Our conclusion from the moral point of view must be hypothetical in form: if decision-making within the ICC is typically utilitarian in these aspects, and if these aspects of utilitarianism constitute moral deficiencies in this particular context, then the deci-

158

sion-making of the ICC is deficient in these respects. At best we have found that normative thinking within the Commission tends to deemphasize considerations of equity and tends to limit unduly the range of persons it considers in reaching its decisions. The purpose of making this known is neither to praise nor to admonish the Commission. It is rather to underscore aspects of the Commission's normative thinking that might under some circumstances constitute shortcomings, so that reflective persons concerned with the affairs of the Commission might gain a better understanding of its potential weaknesses.

A morally sound agent is one at least who is aware of his potential shortcomings, and exercises particular caution in practical circumstances where these shortcomings threaten to influence his decision-making. A few possible circumstances of this character came into view during the course of our analysis of ICC thinking, which we will briefly describe in the interests of reflective self-examination on the part of the regulators.

By mandate, the ICC is responsible to the people of Illinois, and by its conception of "long term" issues is effectively limited in its concern to members of the present generation. On the other hand, substantial majorities of the regulators sampled felt strongly that the future well-being of our nation requires curtailing current patterns of growth in energy consumption (Table 5.2), and comparable numbers rejected the proposal that less attention ought to be given in the future to environmental matters. This indicates a clear inclination to extend their concern both geographically and temporally beyond the here-and-now which their mandate dictates. On a less conjectural level, it is becoming abundantly apparent that the handling and processing of nuclear fuel to which a large majority of regulators appear committed in their endorsement of nuclear plants in Illinois (Table 5.2(k)) involves consequences both outside the state of Illinois (in the transportation of radioactive materials and in widespread danger from possible nuclear accidents) and beyond the present generation (in storage and processing of waste materials). The implication clearly seems to be that exclusive concern with the well-being of the citizens of Illinois is in fact too restrictive. In view of this tension

159

between the rather severely limited geographical and temporal concern imposed by the mandate and the considerably more extensive range of concern to which most of the regulators seem inclined in their thinking, the ICC might consider establishing an office with the explicit responsibility of assessing the effects of Commission decisions beyond the immediate present and outside of Illinois.

A second area of practical decision-making in which the normative configuration found in the ICC might have debilitating consequences is one in which the interests of the utilities come into direct conflict with the interests of the public at large. An instructive example is afforded by the recent accident at Three Mile Island, with the ensuing problem of who is to pay for the clean-up and replacement of the damaged facility. Should the costs be borne primarily by the private investors--an option that would severely damage the financial structure of the utility? Or should they be borne primarily by the rate-paying public--an option that seems unfair since the public was in no way responsible? If a similar issue were to arise within the ICC's jurisdiction, a sharp tension could be set up between the utilitarian and the "equal claim" modes of thinking which already exist within the Commission. Utilitarian thinking might advocate, on one side, that the interests of the utilites (including investors) should be subordinate to the interests of the public at large, and that the Commission could not expect the public to provide bail for the company. "Equal claim" thinking, on the other side, might judge (as in a court decision) that the company has interests that ought to be protected in their right, and that the public will have to absorb the higher rates that are necessary if the company is to continue to make power available. Although the internal structure of the ICC does not seem to encourage prospects of relieving all tension between the dual roles its members play of advocate and judge, future attempts at self-examination within the Commission might do well to continue efforts of the recent past to sort these functions out and to keep them separate (Dowling, 1976).

Yet another area of possible future concern is suggested by the strong indications appearing in our data that a majority of the respondents are very much

160

aware of our nation's impending energy shortage and
are actively thinking about appropriate modes of response. Among these indications are the strong agreement that our growth rates of energy consumption
should be curtailed in the future (Tables 5.2(c-e)),
and the overwhelming support given to the proposition
that the ICC should encourage the use of solar energy
within its jurisdiction (Table 5.2(1)). This senti-
ment was accompanied by a general rejection of the
free-market as an adequate mechanism for adapting
the power wants to the power needs of the consuming
public (Tables 5.3(d and f)). It would seem to follow that, in the Commission's opinion, regulatory or
other governmental influence must be exercised to
help the public adjust its consumption rates to acceptable levels. Yet an implicit suggestion that industry or government ought to become involved in efforts to influence how the public spends its available
income was almost unanimously rejected by our group
of respondents. On the face of it, at least, this
set of attitudes appears inconsistent. To the extent
that the near consensus of the ICC that energy con-
servation ought to be among its goals is genuine--and
there is no reason to doubt the genuineness of our
indications--then its planners might want to re-exam-
ine what appears to be an opposing consensus that the
Commission not become involved in efforts to influence
public energy-use patterns.

NOTE

1. A close examination of Table 7.2 suggests
that the absence of statistically significant differences between the ICC and the utility executives on
the CLGES (and the norms as well) is less a function
of the regulators' average scores than of the greater
diversity within the ICC sample, as indicated by the
relatively large standard deviations. The standard
deviations also are high for the Allport test. Both
the "mediating" position mentioned above and the consensus discussed in Chapter Five thus may be due more
to variety than to blandness of viewpoint.

161

CONCLUSIONS

REFERENCES

Allport, G.W., Vernon, P.E., and Lindzey, G. (1970), _Study of Values_, Third Edition, Houghton Mifflin Co., Boston.

Hahn, M.E. (1969), _The California Life Goals Evaluation Schedules_, Western Psychological Services, Los Angeles.

Sayre, K.M. (ed.) (1977), _Values in the Electric Power Industry_, University of Notre Dame Press, Notre Dame, Indiana.

TABLE 7.1

Mean Scores on Allport Study of Values,
ICC Respondents Compared with Utility Executives

Interest area	ICC (n=44)		Utilities[a] (n=48)		Difference-of-means tests (t)	
	Mean rank	Std. dev.	Mean rank	Std. dev.	ICC vs. Util.	Util. vs. Norms
Theoretical	40.68	9.30	45.22	6.38	-2.68***	5.83****
Economic	42.50	11.96	46.25	6.64	-1.82*	6.06*****
Aesthetic	38.09	10.31	36.66	7.30	0.75	-2.07*
Social	35.25	10.34	33.16	7.35	1.10	-5.94*****
Political	42.30	9.92	39.43	6.39	1.62	-1.02
Religious	36.66	11.31	39.50	9.22	-1.30	-1.12

*p < .05
***p < .005
*****p < .0005
aSayre, 1977, p. 172

163

TABLE 7.2

Mean Scores on CLGES,
ICC Respondents Compared with Utility Executives

Life goal	ICC (n=43)		Utilities[a] (n=49)		Difference-of-means tests (t)	
	Mean rank	Std. dev.	Mean rank	Std. dev.	ICC vs. Util.	Util. vs. Norms
Esteem	29.2	7.1	29.3	5.2	-0.08	-7.24***
Profit	30.7	7.7	33.8	6.0	-2.11*	4.24****
Fame	22.5	5.7	22.9	4.7	-0.36	2.56**
Power	23.2	5.7	22.3	5.0	0.79	0.39
Leadership	35.2	7.4	36.3	5.0	-0.81	4.34***
Security	27.2	6.2	26.2	6.1	0.77	-1.96*
Social service	26.0	7.4	25.1	6.7	0.60	-2.87**
Interest. exp.	32.4	7.4	33.8	5.3	-1.02	2.26*
Self-express.	33.7	6.8	32.1	5.0	1.26	1.45
Independence	29.3	6.6	27.6	5.5	1.32	-1.70*
Correction factor	+3.4		+2.4			

*p<.05 **p<.01 ***p<.001

[a]Sayre, 1977, pp. 175-177; compared with norms, as presented in Table 4.4

Appendix A

Occupational Patterns of Past Commissioners

Our primary focus in this study has been upon ICC commissioners and staff serving as of June, 1977. To test the suggestion that regulators often are drawn from the ranks of regulated industry and return to these ranks after their terms of service, however, we attempted to locate documented career information on all past Commissioners appointed after 1940. We were sucessful in the cases of twenty out of twenty-eight such persons. Tables A-1 and A-2 summarize the affiliations of these persons before and after service on the ICC.

We found evidence of direct or indirect (e.g., lawyer-client) prior association between commissioners and regulated utilities in three (or 15 percent) of the cases, and the same number of associations subsequent to ICC service. Associations of either sort were possible in a number of other cases, but there was no evidence to show that it existed. If we were to assume that every law firm or bank with which the commissioners were involved had utility clients, we would get a maximum of thirteen (or 65 percent) of the commissioners with prior contacts and eight (47 percent) with subsequent contacts. In fact, it would appear likely that considerably fewer than half of the past commissioners had prior or subsequent professional ties with the industries they regulated. Further, we found little reason to suspect that the contacts actually documented were in any way improper. In particular, it appears that very few of the documented contacts involved relationships with utility companies under the ICC's jurisdiction.

TABLE A-1

Occupations of ICC Commissioners Prior
to ICC Appointment

Occupational setting	N[*]	%
Government[+]	15	75
Private law practice	12	60
Business[++]	9	45
Journalism	2	10
Academic institutions	1	5
ICC staff	1	5

[*]Totals greater than 20 (100 percent) because of multiple affiliations in some cases.

[+]Federal, state and local, and in all branches of government.

[++]Including four in banking.

TABLE A-2

Occupations of ICC Commissioners
After Leaving the Commission

Occupational setting	N*	%**
Private law practice	7	41
Government	4	24
Business	3	18
Academic institutions	2	12
Died in office or retired	4	24
Still serving on ICC	3	-

*Total greater than 20 (100 percent) because of multiple affiliations in some cases.

**Percentages exclude those currently still serving on the Commission.

Appendix B
Questionnaires Used in Study

QUESTIONNAIRE
ON
VALUES AND THE REGULATION OF ELECTRIC POWER

PREPARED FOR COMPLETION BY COMMISSIONERS & STAFF OF THE
ILLINOIS COMMERCE COMMISSION

General Instructions:

This questionnaire consists of 16 separate parts, each of them a page or two in length. Some parts will ask you simply to check a response, while others are open-ended, calling for answers in a few words or in a short paragraph. In content, the items will range from simple informational or opinion questions to more complex questions calling for some reflection.

The specific instructions for each section appear at the beginning of that section. Because the questionnaire is quite long, you may want to complete it in parts, rather than all at one sitting. While there is a logical progression from part to part, the order is not of great importance, so you can feel free to alter it if you wish. We do ask, however, that you answer every part as fully as possible.

Some sections explicitly ask for or suggest explanatory or clarifying comments and provide space for these. Whether comments are specifically requested or not, you are encouraged to add them whenever you feel inclined to do so. These comments will be of great value to us as we go about the task of interpreting the responses. If the space provided is insufficient, feel free to use the reverse side of the pages or to add additional sheets.

APPENDIX B

I. Background Information

Name _____   Title _____

Age: _____   Sex: ____ M ____ F   Member of ethnic/racial minority: ____Yes ____No

Political preference: ____Republican ____ Democrat ____ Other: _____

Educational background:

Colleges or universities attended	Dates	Major field(s)	Degree

Occupational History: starting with your current position

Employer	Position	Dates

Approximately what percentage of your time is devoted to work related to the regulation of electric power? _____%

Please give a brief, but specific, description of your duties with the ICC:

Name of your immediate superior at ICC: _____

Which of the following comes closest to describing your occupation at present:
____ lawyer ____ accountant ____ engineer ____ administrator ____ scientist
____ other _____

How did you come to be associated with the ICC? (check all that apply)

____ published advertisement   ____ competitive examination
____ personal contact with commissioner or staff member ____ other: _____
____ political appointment
____ college recruitment process   _____.

What are your future career plans/hopes if and when you leave the ICC?

II. Here are a number of statements, general principles concerning regulation, public welfare, and the economy. In the space provided, please indicate whether you tend to agree or to disagree with each statement. Use the space below each statement for any clarifications or comments you may wish to make.

	Strongly Agree	Agree	Disagree	Strongly Disagree
1. A good decision is one which results in the most benefit for the greatest number of persons.	____	____	____	____
2. The public is best served by the pursuit of enlightened self-interest by private industry.	____	____	____	____
3. The consumer should be free to spend his income as he chooses, with as little dictation from business or government as possible.	____	____	____	____
4. The initiative for changes in business policies which impinge directly on the public welfare should come from regulatory bodies; it is not the place of business to take the initiative in these matters.	____	____	____	____
5. While regulation may be necessary in some specific instances, the market place is the best protector of the general public interest in meeting our long term needs for abundant energy.	____	____	____	____

	Strongly Agree	Agree	Disagree	Strongly Disagree

6. There is no sense in discussing hypothetical situations or changes--the law is the law and that's that.

7. The business of business is profit, not justice or the betterment of society; the business of regulation is justice and the betterment of society.

8. The regulation of utilities should reflect the philosophy that regulation is necessary because society as a whole benefits from an insured supply of energy and would be harmed by an economic decision to withhold supply.

9. Regulation should attempt to approximate the supply and price that would exist if energy were not provided by monopolies.

10. The free market system can not adequately represent the interests of future generations in preserving energy sources and environmental amenities.

11. The obligations of businessmen and regulators alike are to current constituencies; they cannot reasonably be asked to take the needs of future generations into account in their decision-making.

171

	Strongly Agree	Agree	Disagree	Strongly Disagree

12. In the future we ought to define progress more in terms of an improved quality of life than in terms of growth in the GNP.

13. In contemporary society, business managers must recognize responsibilities to many constituencies (e.g., employees, customers, the public at large), not just to their stockholders.

14. The level of market demand for a good is the only feasible way of measuring the need for that good; if there is a high level of demand for electric power, we must assume that people need that much power.

15. The growth in size of utility firms is generally of benefit to society; the larger the firm is, the more it will benefit from economies of scale, thereby producing energy more efficiently and cheaply.

16. When an individual acts in his role within an organization, he must act according to the policies of that organization and not according to his own private view, if different.

172

III. The next set of statements are opinions on some current practical questions drawn from a variety of published and other sources. Following the same directions as in the previous section, indicate whether you agree or disagree with each statement.

	Strongly Agree	Agree	Disagree	Strongly Disagree
1. Items such as air conditioning have become virtually indispensible to a moderate standard of living in this country.	_____	_____	_____	_____
2. When it comes down to it, there are really very few important decisions which a utility company is free to make, given the regulated nature of the industry.	_____	_____	_____	_____
3. The well-being of our society requires that we give less attention in the future to purely environmental matters than we have in the recent past.	_____	_____	_____	_____
4. Although there are some exceptions, most intervenors are motivated by a sincere concern for the well-being of society.	_____	____	_____	_____
5. The rate of growth in electrical consumption must slow down; we cannot continue doubling electrical consumption every decade.	_____	_____	_____	_____

	Strongly Agree	Agree	Disagree	Strongly Disagree
6. The future well-being of our nation demands that we curtail the growth of our overall energy consumption.	_____	_____	_____	_____
7. The energy policies of the Carter Administration are basically sound, a move in the right direction.	_____	_____	_____	_____
8. Utility company representatives generally have the advantage over commission staff in presenting the facts relating to cases concerning the electric power industry.	_____	_____	_____	_____
9. The so-called energy crisis isn't really a crisis at all; there's plenty of energy available for all our needs now and in the foreseeable future.	_____	_____	_____	_____
10. Nuclear power is currently the safest and most practical answer to our nation's energy needs.	_____	_____	_____	_____
11. Given the present legal and political structure, the regulatory commission has relatively little room for discretion in the decisions it makes.	_____	_____	_____	_____

APPENDIX B

	Strongly Agree	Agree	Disagree	Strongly Disagree

12. Generally speaking, most utility executives are honest, public-spirited citizens who are sincerely concerned about the public welfare.

13. The ICC should make extensive attempts to eliminate social inequities by assuming the role of principal advocate for low income consumers as part of its regulatory function.

14. The ICC should actively encourage the use of solar energy within its jurisdiction.

The work of the ICC is generally supported by:

15. The Governor

16. The Legislature

17. Utility Companies

18. The General Public

175

APPENDIX B

IV. Please indicate whether you agree or disagree with each of the following statements, as they apply to your experience with the ICC as an organization.

	Strongly Agree	Agree	Disagree	Strongly Disagree
1. Most decisions are fairly routine, based on past decisions of the same type.				
2. There are clearly established procedures for arriving at decisions on particular problems.				
3. The hierarchy of responsibility in the Commission is clearly defined.				
4. It is often hard to get things done because of the amount of red tape involved.				
5. Decisions are made on an ad hoc basis, rather than according to established priorities and policies.				
6. The orientation of new staff members is generally adequate.				
7. Salaries, benefits and working conditions are generally good enough to attract and retain high quality personnel.				
8. Lower echelon personnel are routinely involved in discussions of significant decisions.				
9. Working with the ICC has been a personally satisfying experience.				

V. In the following section there are a number of broad questions presented, along
    with a list of possible alternative answers to each question. Please check the
    alternative which you personally find most acceptable.

    Then in the space below the list, please explain briefly why you prefer this
    alternative.

1. What sort of base load generating facilities ought to be built in Illinois in
    the foreseeable future?

    __ only nuclear plants
    __ only coal-fired plants
    __ only oil-fired plants
    __ a mixture of all the above types of plants
    __ other: _____

    Why do you prefer this alternative?

2. What should be the pattern of growth in electric power use in Illinois in the
    future?

    __ more rapid growth than at present
    __ continued growth at the present rate
    __ continued growth, but at a slower rate than at present
    __ zero growth--maintaining electric power use at current levels
    __ negative growth--reduction in the amount of electric power use
    __ other: _____

    Why do you prefer this alternative?

3. Which of the following policies should be adopted regarding the allowability
    of sales and advertising expenses in rate cases?

    __ all sales and advertising expenses should be allowed
    __ more than half of these expenses should be allowed
    __ less than half of these expenses should be allowed
    __ none of these expenses should be allowed
    __ other: _____

    Why do you prefer this alternative?

4. What should be the policy for determining the order in which the processing of rate cases is completed?

___ cases should be completed in the order in which they are filed
___ cases where the utility is experiencing financial operating difficulties should be completed first
___ cases of utilities which have sought rate increases the least frequently should be completed first
___ cases of the larger utilities should be completed first
___ cases of the smaller utilities should be completed first
___ other: _____

Why do you prefer this alternative?

5. What do you feel should be the comparison between the allowable rates of return for electric and gas utilities?

___ electric utilities should be allowed slightly higher rates of return than gas utilities
___ electric utilities and gas utilities should be allowed the same rate of return
___ electric utilities should be allowed slightly lower rates of return than gas utilities
___ other: _____

Why do you prefer this alternative?

6. What do you feel should be the comparison among the rate levels for residential, commercial and industrial rate schedules for the same amount of kwh used?

___ higher rates for residential customers than for commercial and industrial customers
___ same rates for residential, commercial and industrial customers
___ lower rates for residential customers than for c mmercial and industrial customers
___ other: _____

Why do you prefer this alternative?

7. How can electric utilities best establish rate schedules to reflect the costs incurred in providing electric service to:

A. Residential customers
___ simple charge for kwh used only
___ separate charges for kwh used and kw demand (multi-part rates)
___ flat customer charge per month only (similar to telephone billings)
___ other: _____

B. Commercial customers
    __ simple charge for kwh used only
    __ separate charges for kwh used and kw demand (multi-part rates)
    __ flat customer charge per month only (similar to telephone billings)
    __ other: _____

C. Industrial customers
    __ simple charge for kwh used only
    __ separate charges for kwh used and kw demand (multi-part rates)
    __ flat customer charge per month only (similar to telephone billings)
    __ other: _____

Why do you prefer these alternatives?

8. If charges for kwh and/or kw demand remain incorporated in electric utility
    rate schedules which of the following rate designs do you prefer for:

A. Residential customers
    __ declining block rates
    __ flat rates
    __ inverted rates
    __ other: _____

B. Commercial customers
    __ declining block rates
    __ flat rates
    __ inverted rates
    __ other: _____

C. Industrial customers
    __ declining block rates
    __ flat rates
    __ inverted rates
    __ other: _____

Why do you prefer these alternatives?

9. What, in your judgment, is the ultimate criterion generally operative in ICC decision making for deciding what is or is not in the public interest?

   __(a) what the majority of the public wants (e.g., as expressed in a Gallup poll)

   __(b) what the public wants, as expressed in the will of governmental representatives (which, specifically? _____)

   __(c) what the ICC commissioners finally and reflectively prefer

   __(d) whatever would be chosen by a unanimously acceptable procedure

   __(e) what would make the majority of people happiest

   __(f) what the majority of both public interest groups and public utilities would find acceptable

   __(g) what would most contribute to social and environmental stability

   __(h) what the free market would allow to prevail

   __(i) a combination of these (specify by letter in rank order: _____)

   __(j) other: _____

Is this the criterion you personally believe should be used? __yes __no

If no, what criterion should be used?

VI. Here is a list of hypothetical changes from current public policy with regard to the electric power industry and its regulation. Please indicate whether you would approve or disapprove of each of these changes. In the space below each item, please feel free to explain your response or to make any comments you may wish to make.

	Strongly Approve	Approve	Disapprove	Strongly Disapprove
1. Standardization of the process by which power plants are licensed to operate.	_____	_____	_____	_____
2. Providing for public input at a much earlier point in the nuclear licensing process.	_____	_____	_____	_____
3. Greater control of nuclear-plant licensing by state regulatory commissions.	_____	_____	_____	_____
4. Repeal of the National Environmental Policy Act (NEPA).	_____	_____	_____	_____
5. Nationalization of all electric utilities.	_____	_____	_____	_____
6. General deregulation of all electric utilities.	_____	_____	_____	_____
7. Deregulation of utility rate structures and levels.	_____	_____	_____	_____

APPENDIX B

		Strongly Approve	Approve	Disapprove	Strongly Disapprove
8.	Selection of future generating facility sites by state agencies.				
9.	Requirement of regional, rather than site-by-site environmental impact assessment.				
10.	Giving the utilities discretion to resist the growth of power demand in their service areas.				
11.	Development of alternatives to the adversary process in utility regulation.				
12.	Creation of separate state regulatory commissions for different types of public utilities.				
13.	Transfer of all utility regulation to the federal level.				
14.	Election of regulatory commissioners.				
15.	Longer terms of office for commissioners.				
16.	Permitting Commission staff to appeal Commission decisions in court.				

182

VII. Considering each of the following types of authority, please indicate whether, as you understand the law, the ICC now has that authority, some other government agency has it, or no government agency has it.

Then indicate what agency, if any, ought to have that authority, whether or not it currently exists. If you mark any of the starred columns, please name the agency involved, using the space provided at the right.

Authority:	Actually Vested In:				Ought to be Vested In:				Agency Name
	ICC*	Other State/ Local Agency*	Federal Agency*	No Gov't Agency	ICC*	Other State/ Local Agency*	Federal Agency*	No Gov't Agency	
1. To initiate electric rates.									
2. To disallow a rate structure that will yield more than a reasonable profit.									
3. To disallow a rate structure that will be insufficient to meet current maintenance requirements.									
4. To determine whether a company's future capital needs are to be met out of current profits or whether they will require new external funding.									
5. To choose between alternative ratemaking theories (e.g., "prudent investment," replacement cost, etc.).									
6. To require an electric company to adopt a rate structure that will discourage the wasteful use of electricity (forbid quantity discounts, require off-peak discounts, etc.).									
7. To determine whether facilities shall be expanded to meet increased or anticipated demand for services.									
8. To determine what kind of new facilities a company may adopt (nuclear, fossil fuel, hydroelectric, etc.).									

183

Authority:	Actually Vested In:				Ought to be Vested In:				Agency Name
	ICC *	Other State/ Local Agency	Federal Agency	No Gov't Agency	ICC *	Other State/ Local Agency *	Federal Agency *	No Gov't Agency	
9. To pass on the siting and design of new facilities.									
10. To distribute territory and customers between electric companies.									
11. To adopt an overall energy policy applicable to the state.									
12. To control growth in supply of specific energy types (e.g., gas vs. electric vs. oil vs. solar).									
Other types of authority you feel to be of particular interest:									
13. _____									
14. _____									

184

VIII. The following is a list of factors which seem likely to have an impact on the regulatory process. For each of these factors, please indicate how significant an impact it generally has on (a) your own work with the Commission and (b) the work of the Commission as a whole.

Then, considering only those factors which you have marked "highly significant," rank these according to their relative importance, with "1" being most significant.

	Impact on Your Own Work			Impact on Work of Whole Commission		
	Of little/ no signif.	Moder- ately signif.	Highly signif- icant	Rank	Of little/ no signif.	Moder- ately signif.	Highly signif- icant	Rank
1. Public Opinion								
2. Existing laws								
3. Political pressure								
4. Judicial interpretations								
5. Prevailing attitudes of Commis- sioners and/or staff								
6. Existing administrative proce- dures in the Commission.								
7. Time pressure								
8. Inadequate financial resources								
9. Geographical or other physical arrangements of the Commission								
10. Need to maintain good relations with utility companies								
11. Need to maintain good relations with intervenor groups								
12. Personal beliefs, conscience								
13. Other: _____								

185

IX. Insofar as the ICC represents many different constituencies, it is likely that the commissioners and staff receive informational input from a wide variety of sources. The list below suggests a number of different potential sources of influence on your thinking about questions of regulation. Please indicate the approximate frequency of contact you personally have with each type of input listed, as well as your best estimate of the frequency of contact for the Commission as a whole. Use the blank spaces provided to list any other similar contacts which you feel should be included. Note: in this section we are concerned only with the amount of contact, not with the extent to which it is actually influential.

Type Of Input	Approximate Frequency For Yourself					Approximate Frequency For The Commission As A Whole (your best estimate)				
	more than once a week	once a week	once a month	less than once a month	never or almost never	more than once a week	once a week	once a month	less than once a month	never or almost never
1. Conversations with other ICC personnel	—	—	—	—	—	—	—	—	—	—
2. Conversations with relatives or personal friends	—	—	—	—	—	—	—	—	—	—
3. Contacts with members or staff of other regulatory bodies	—	—	—	—	—	—	—	—	—	—
4. Contacts with state legislators	—	—	—	—	—	—	—	—	—	—
5. Formal visits by utility representatives	—	—	—	—	—	—	—	—	—	—
6. Informal contacts (e.g., lunches) with utility representatives.	—	—	—	—	—	—	—	—	—	—
7. Formal visits by intervenors	—	—	—	—	—	—	—	—	—	—
8. Informal contacts with intervenors	—	—	—	—	—	—	—	—	—	—
9. Other personal contacts: _____ _____	—	—	—	—	—	—	—	—	—	—

Type Of Input	Approximate Frequency For Yourself						Approximate Frequency For The Commission As A Whole (your best estimate)					
	more than once a week	once a week	once a month	less than once a month	never or almost never		more than once a week	once a week	once a month	less than once a month	never or almost never	
10. Trade journals (e.g., Public Utility Fortnightly, etc.)	—	—	—	—	—		—	—	—	—	—	
11. Newspapers, radio, TV, popular magazines	—	—	—	—	—		—	—	—	—	—	
12. Memos or "white papers" from utilities	—	—	—	—	—		—	—	—	—	—	
13. Legislative memos	—	—	—	—	—		—	—	—	—	—	
14. Other sources: _____												
_____	—	—	—	—	—		—	—	—	—	—	

Of all the inputs just listed, which do you find most important as influence(s) on your own thinking about regulation?

It is possible that you encounter a potential source of information with some frequency, but that you do not regard it as having any significant influence on your thinking. If there are any such sources listed, which are they?

187

Are there any of these inputs which you find problematic, or about which you have any reservations, ethically, politically, or in any other way? If so, please explain which input and what you consider to be problematic about it:

Please list the two or three books or other materials which you would consider the best sources for an understanding of the regulatory process:

1.

2.

3.

In the space below, please list any industry or professional journals which you read fairly regularly:

1.

2.

3.

Here, please list any recent books or other materials which you feel have had a major impact on your own values about public policy (e.g., regarding energy, environment, etc.)

1.

2.

3.

X. Please read the following statement of the general theory behind regulation.
If it does not accurately reflect your own view of regulation, please critique
it and explain how it should read.

"Regulation of certain industries is necessary because these industries
tend toward monopoly, insofar as the firms in these industries operate most
efficiently under monopolistic conditions. In the absence of the free market
mechanisms which handle the problems of allocation and pricing, regulation
exists to insure to the public non-discriminatory access to service at reasonable cost, while also securing reasonable rates of return to the providers of
service."

Check here if this statement is adequate ____

In your own words, how would you describe the central responsibility or mandate
of a regulated electric power company?

What is the specific source of this mandate?

In the context of electric power, what would you say is the central responsibility
or mandate of the Illinois Commerce Commission?

XI. Decisions are sometimes referred to as "short-run" or "near-term" or "long-range," or the like. Roughly speaking, how long a time span would you be thinking of if you were to use the following expressions in the context of your work:

      1. "Short-run" _____ years

      2. "Long-run" _____ years

XII. Considering all aspects of decision-making about electric power, how would you rate the overall performance of each of the following: (Place an X on each scale at the point which corresponds to your rating.)

1. The electric utility industry
   as a whole

    10   5   0
    Highest   Lowest

2. Regulated electric power
   companies in Illinois

    10   5   0

3. Non-regulated (e.g., municipal)
   power companies in Illinois

    10   5   0

4. The Illinois Commerce
   Commissioners

    10   5   0

5. The ICC professional staff

    10   5   0

6. State regulatory commissions in
   general, throughout the country

    10   5   0

7. Federal regulatory agencies

    10   5   0

XIII. Here are a number of adjectives which may or may not be appropriate in describing the ICC as an organization. The adjectives are arranged in contrasting pairs. Between each pair, put an X on the line at the point where you would locate the ICC.

Example: (with "snow" in place of "ICC")

```
                                              X
hot                                          cold
```

1.
```
strong                          weak
```

2.
```
formal                         informal
```

3.
```
swift                           slow
```

4.
```
honest                        dishonest
```

5.
```
sloppy                          neat
```

6.
```
logical                        intuitive
```

7.
```
foolish                         wise
```

8.
```
fat                             lean
```

9.
```
conservative               liberal
```

10.
```
energetic                       tired
```

11.
```
flexible                        rigid
```

12.
```
young                            old
```

13.
```
warm                            cold
```

14.
```
thoughtful                   impetuous
```

XIV. In the space below, please describe a typical problem which you deal with in your own job, and the way in which it would ordinarily be resolved. Please mention any other offices or persons who would normally be involved in the decision-making process, as well as the length of time it would ordinarily take to resolve the issue. (Continue on the reverse side of this page if necessary.)

191

In any field of activity there are likely to be particular situations which
are special sources of difficulty or situations which present special
decision-making challenges. (For example, those in the field of education
may find the assignment of grades particularly difficult; law enforcement
officers may see special problems in following civil rights procedures in
some arrests, etc.). In the space below, please describe one or more
situations which you feel are specially problematic or challenging for the
ICC decision-making or for regulatory decisions in general.

What do you like most and least about the Illinois Commerce Commission?

    Most:

    Least:

What do you like most and least about your own work with the ICC?

    Most:

    Least:

If you were in a position to make any changes from the present way in which
electric power is regulated in Illinois--changes in laws, procedures,
attitudes, anything--what specific changes would you make?

XV. There are things about every person which are not readily forced into check-
lists. In the space below, please tell us a little more about yourself,
including any of these or similar types of information which you feel
describe you as a person: family background; ethnic, religious or fraternal
associations; political or civic activities; concerns about public issues
(e.g., environment, consumer affairs, gun control, abortion, capital punishment, etc.); hobbies and leisure activities.

What, in your estimation, are the three most critical problems facing America today? (Please list in descending order of importance.)

1.

2.

3.

XVI.   Are there any other comments you would like to add--about the ICC, about regulation, about the content of this questionnaire, or about this study in general?

APPENDIX B

on

VALUES AND THE REGULATION OF ELECTRIC POWER

General Instructions: In the following pages you will find a set of
eight stories or scenarios having to do with
the regulation of electric power. In these
scenarios you will find brief descriptions of
problems faced by various decision-makers--
utility executives, regulators, legislators--all
concerned with electric power. At the end of each
story, you are asked to give your own opinion of
the decision reached, as well as the reasons which
have led you to form this opinion.

Some of the situations are similar to actual cases;
others are more hypothetical, though an attempt has
been made to avoid radically implausible assumptions.

It should be stressed that none of the decisions is
obviously correct or incorrect, good or bad. All of
the scenarios involve issues on which persons of intelligence and good will may disagree.

In responding to each scenario, please accept the
"facts" of the case as given, as far as possible, and
focus instead on the principles which you feel are
relevant to the situation and the assumptions which
appear to be involved.

195

APPENDIX B

Valleyview Public Service Company has agreed to provide more needed power to an isolated mountain community in its service area. Their initial plan was to build a small plant to be fueled by low-grade coal mined locally, rather than string lines from a large new plant a considerable distance away over extremely rugged terrain.

As a result of the community's past involvement in the coal industry, there are an unusually large number of persons with chronic lung diseases in the area. Supported by their local physician and the public health service, they have petitioned out of court that the company not construct the local plant, on the grounds that their health would be further endangered by stack emissions even low enough to satisfy the EPA.

Given the community's economic condition, more electric power and jobs are definitely needed. Moreover, bringing the power across the mountains probably would result in higher rates than if it were produced locally.

The officers of Valleyview Public Service have concluded that the utility can fulfill its obligation to serve the area in either way without financial penalty to itself. After weighing the various arguments, they have decided to abandon construction plans and prepare to string the power lines across the mountains.

* * * * *

What is your personal opinion of their decision?

_____strongly agree _____agree _____disagree _____strongly disagree

Please explain the reasoning underlying your opinion:

APPENDIX B

Scenario II

Regional Power Company had planned to build a new nuclear generating facility which was scheduled to come on line in ten years, but recent changes in the economy and public attitudes toward energy use have caused the company to re-evaluate that decision.

According to the finance department, the cost of financing the unit is at the highest level in years. It is highly uncertain whether the financial picture will improve or worsen in the next few years.

The statistical department has submitted two very different load forecasts. According to one set of assumptions, the new capacity will definitely be needed in order to assure reliability in 1985 and after. The other assumptions suggest that current capacity should be sufficient, although with a somewhat lower reserve margin than is usual.

Taking all these points into consideration, the officers of Regional Power have decided to postpone the construction of the nuclear unit indefinitely.

* * * * *

What is your personal opinion of their decision?

_____strongly agree   _____agree   _____disagree   _____strongly disagree

Please explain the reasoning underlying your opinion:

197

Enterprise Electric Company serves a predominantly rural region. The local Chamber of Commerce is considering whether to encourage construction of a highly automated steel plant in their area.

Enterprise's generating facilities currently are operating below capacity. The new steel plant would raise its base load to near optimal level.

An economic impact analysis has indicated that the net gain in jobs in the area would be fairly small. Further, the new tax revenues would be counter-balanced by the cost of additional services required. Also, an environmental impact analysis indicates that, even after treatment, the steel plant's stack emissions would increase the level of air pollution considerably (though not beyond the legal limits).

The Board of Directors of Enterprise Electric, after reviewing the plans and reports, has directed the Chairman to use his influence with the Chamber of Commerce members, in order to secure a decision in favor of the steel plant.

* * * * *

What is your personal opinion of their decision?

_____strongly agree   _____agree   _____disagree   _____strongly disagree

Please explain the reasoning underlying your opinion:

APPENDIX B

Scenario IV

A bill is gaining support in Congress which would in large measure deregulate investor-owned utilities, allowing them to operate for the most part as free enterprise operations.

According to the proposed law, utilities would no longer be granted exclusive territorial franchises, nor would their rates be subject to regulatory agency approval, with one exception: residential users would be entitled to have some utility assigned to afford them minimum or "lifeline" services at regulated rates. In other respects utility business affairs would be conducted in the same fashion as those of other industries, and utility service would be a matter of negotiation between utility and user. Public health and safety laws would remain in effect.

* * * * *

What is your personal opinion of this legislative proposal?

_____strongly agree   _____agree   _____disagree   _____strongly disagree

Please explain the reasoning underlying your opinion:

Scenario V

Several serious floods in past years have demonstrated the need for a flood control project in the Cowlick River valley. The Army Corps of Engineers (ACE) proposes to build a dam on Cowlick River for flood control and for hydroelectric power. Option to construct and to operate the generating facility has been offered to Local Power and Light, which needs added generating capacity for its expansion program.

Suit to block the project has been filed on behalf of an Amish community whose land would be flooded by the dam lake. The Amish farmers claim that their loss in property, agricultural productivity and cultural heritage could not be adequately compensated under eminent domain, and that the building of the dam means the destruction of their way of life.

After considerable reflection, the officers of the utility have decided to file a brief in court supporting the ACE in the suit.

* * * * *

What is your personal opinion of their decision?

_____strongly agree   _____agree   _____disagree   _____strongly disagree

Please explain the reasoning underlying your opinion:

Scenario VI

The load projection department of Smithtown Power and Light Company had presented a forecast which suggested the need for increased base load capacity
in the next decades. At the meeting of the company officers called to
discuss this forecast, the following alternatives were discussed: (1) to make
immediate plans to build a new 700 MWe plant, and (2) to explore the possibility
of meeting demand through the purchase of power from other utilities in the
region.

After considerable and heated debate, the Senior Vice-President, who had been
generally silent up to this point, spoke up: "Gentlemen, it seems to me that
we are ignoring one alternative which should at least be considered: we could
attempt to lower the demand for power enough to allow us to meet it with our
existing capacity. I've been studying these figures and it seems that most of
the increase is due to that new industrial complex planned in Deep Hollow.
Now if we were to work with the developer there, I'm willing to bet we could
come up with some ideas to keep their electric use way down. And if we could
get our present customers to do the same, we wouldn't need that extra capacity."

His suggestion failed to generate any notable support from the rest of the
group. In the end the company decided to go ahead with the plans for the new
construction.

* * * * *

What is your personal opinion of their decision?

_____strongly agree   _____agree   _____disagree   _____strongly disagree

Please explain the reasoning underlying your opinion:

201

APPENDIX B

Scenario VII

A heated debate has arisen at the West Carolina Commerce Commission as a consequence of a recent rate increase request by Consolidated Power (the state's largest and most advanced electric utility). As a result of certain significant changes in Consolidated's management philosophy, the firm has embraced a pair of new and expensive objectives reflected in the rate proposal:

(a) to retrofit several of its major plants with emission control equipment of a higher degree of efficiency than mandated by Federal standards, and

(b) to begin construction of a modest but highly innovative experimental plant which would convert solar energy into electrical energy.

"It's time we led, rather than followed," the managers claimed.

The debate in the Commerce Commission centered around the fairness to ratepayers of reflecting the costs of Consolidated's new ventures in the rate base. Three camps developed in the Commission debate. One camp argued that it was necessary to reward the public spirited actions of Consolidated by allowing the rate increase in this instance, but that promulgating rules to encourage experimentation by utilities would represent undue tampering with managerial independence in the industry. A second camp argued that such a rule ought to be promulgated and that the Commission, as a matter of policy, must redirect the development strategies of the power companies in the state. The third camp insisted that the main function of the Commission was to secure sufficient power for the consumer at the lowest rates consistent with fairness to investors, and that Consolidated's expenses in this case were inconsistent with that function.

The Commissioners finally decided to disallow the increase.

* * * * *

_____strongly agree   _____agree   _____disagree   _____strongly disagree

Please explain the reasoning underlying your opinion:

202

APPENDIX B

Scenario VIII

The chairmanship of the East Dakota Public Utilities Commission has become vacant and the Governor is reviewing candidates for appointment to that position. He has narrowed his choice down to four men:

A is an engineer with a strong scientific background. He is known among his peers as a man of integrity and fairness in dealing with people.

B is an accountant with expertise in cost-benefit analysis. He has published several influential articles on that subject and has done outstanding work as a consultant to several government agencies.

C is a small claims court judge. In a position demanding considerable wisdom and insight, he is notable for his honesty, fairness, and compassion.

D is the successful administrator of a state welfare agency; his creative approaches have made the agency a model for those in other states.

* * * * *

If you were the Governor (granted that you'd want to know much more about all the candidates), what preliminary rank order would you assign them, on the basis of the information given here? (give the letter-name of the candidate)

_____1st Choice _____2d Choice _____3d Choice _____4th Choice

Please explain the reasoning underlying your ranking:

Index